Linda

THE TREE OF KNOWLEDGE

By the Same Author

FICTION
The Seven Ages
Nelly's Version
Light
Waking
Ghosts

NONFICTION
Patriarchal Attitudes

THE
TREE
OF
KNOWLEDGE

EVA FIGES

PANTHEON BOOKS   NEW YORK

Copyright © 1990 by Eva Figes

Conventions. Published in the United States by Pantheon Books, a
division of Random House, Inc., New York. Originally published in
Great Britain by Sinclair-Stevenson Limited, London, in 1990.

Library of Congress Cataloging-in-Publication Data

Figes, Eva.
The tree of knowledge / by Eva Figes.
p. cm.
ISBN 0-394-58765-0
1. Milton, John, 1608–1674, in fiction, drama, poetry, etc.
2. Milton family—Fiction.   I. Title.
PR6056.I46T74   1991
823'.914—dc20   90-52539

Manufactured in the United States of America
First American Edition

THE TREE OF KNOWLEDGE

ONE

PRAY BE SEATED, sir, and pardon such humble surroundings. This room must serve both as schoolroom and for living in, and I fear it is but a shabby place to receive visitors. You see how bare it is, and lacking in comfort, but children make rough work of household chattels, which consoles me for having so few. I endeavour to keep the bare boards clean, and the hearth swept. It is uphill work, with but a child to help me. I teach her gratis in return, her father having not the wherewithal to pay for schooling, but the work wearies her, and then she is not fit for study. Or else I must turn a blind eye to dust in corners, if she is not to be nodding off over her alphabet.

You do me too much honour to say I follow in my father's footsteps. Let me hang your hat on this nail. The walls are but lately whitewashed, so all is clean. This is a poor neighbourhood, and I teach but the rudiments of reading and arithmetic to children who must work their way through the world in humble callings. They will have little need, I fear, of such learning as my father had at his command. If they can but keep accounts, so the shillings flow in faster than they must needs spend the pence, I shall have done them some service, I think. Their parents will consider those few pence well invested, that they must find for me.

Besides, sir, what have I to offer them? I am but a poor weaver's widow, when all is said and done. Think you my father shared his learning with me, being but a woman? Alas, sir, I have more in common with these unkempt, oft hungry children who come to my door, wishing to learn their alphabet and master sums, though not akin by blood, than with my father.

You say I have his features? This is true enough. But a life of hardship gives us other kin, or so I think. Like my neighbours here, I have known want, and worked with my hands. I was taught to make lace, not to hold converse with scholars, or entertain fine gentlemen. And then, sir, I was denied a dowry. Else it might have been otherwise. It was ever likely I should sink in the world.

Would you have me shut the casement? The street is noisy, and the stench which comes from it in summer weather scarce to be endured. I must choose to have the window shut, and so be stifled, or let the breeze blow in, bringing foul odours with it. I will shut it, if it pleases you. No? Then pray, remove your coat. Let us not stand upon ceremony. I am no fine lady, that you should swelter in it. Pray do so, sir. I can lay it along this bench, and the silk will not harm. I can dust it first.

I would not have you think me bitter. I have long since forgiven him. All I have in my heart now is a kind of love, and much sorrow, that there should have been so little of it when he lived. But we cannot undo the past, can we, sir? Those regrets I have are rather for a kingdom of the mind unshared, too little understood, than aught of worldly wealth. So I am poor, and wedded a poor man. Yet he was

2

fond of me, and did ever treat me kindly. Few can say as much.

I teach but the rudiments here. I have but few books, and time is lacking, had I more to share with them. Their parents, being poor, and mostly ignorant, can find but little purpose in reading poesie, or ancient classics either, had I the knowledge of them. And yet I would give them some little pleasure with their tasks, and not mere drudgery. The pill, being sugared, is taken with a will. I try to teach them Christian principles, and open up their minds to such simple delights as they will understand and I am mistress of.

For you must know – my cousin wrote of it – that though I am my father's daughter, he made me not his heir. I speak, sir, not of the dowry denied me, but of the learning in which he was so rich. Had I been his son, that died in infancy the year that I was born, it might have been otherwise. He was, as you have read, schoolmaster to my cousins, Edward and his younger brother John, for many years. They were taught much willynilly, so I was told, and oft went supperless to bed, with nought for their pains but a whipping.

Whether this be a good thing or no, I know not. What think you, sir, that have a scholar's mind? Is this the way to stir the appetite for higher things? My woman's heart says no. And if the consequence should be the judge, it must be said that neither of my cousins rose to greatness, in the manner of my father. Mere hacks of Grub Street, both, and their stepfather, Mr Agar, was much disappointed in them. He thought they had been better served, having no particular gift and no true calling, in the learning of an honest trade. For both died poor, and left the world no better than they found it.

Indeed, my younger cousin was thought to have brought disgrace upon the family, being dissolute of both habit and mind. Is it not strange, sir, that the pupil of such a master should turn out so?

I would not whip my pupils, no. I have not had necessity so to do. And I think I scarce have the strength for it, being old, and a woman. But I think, were I put to it, I would rather send a child away, telling his parents that he wastes their hard-earned pence. The poor cannot afford to keep their children idle, so such a threat would keep them studious.

But to tell the truth, I think my father used my cousins, though his pupils, as his eyes, much as he used my sister and myself. But on account of their sex, and being paid for his services, he did teach them to understand that which they read aloud. My cousin Edward has written of the many ancient authors he and his brother studied whilst in his house. Certainly I have heard him speak of it, with something less than fervour, as a time of hard study and spare diet, the ancient texts being chosen rather to increase my father's knowledge than to inspire young minds. Though he had the use of his eyes then, and might have spared them much tedious matter. 'Tis little wonder, sir, that they would not be obedient without a rod to their backs. I pity the young boy that must needs study Vitruvius, his *Architecture*, or Frontinus, his *Stratagems*. We must whet the appetite with tastier morsels, I think.

As for me, sir, and my sister Mary, it was all one to us, whether the text was dry as dust or heavenly poesie that might have lifted up our spirits, and made us glad. One tongue, he would say, was enough for any woman. And so, his eyes being then quite sightless, we must read to him in many, exactly pronouncing all such foreign tongues as he would have read to him. A task, sir, that must try the patience of a saint, and I was but flesh and blood, and young also.

I see you have brought books with you, to try me. There have been several gentlemen who came to visit me with this purpose, finding it hard to credit such reports. But indeed, sir, 'tis true. I would it had been otherwise. Very well, let us go to it. But my cousin Edward was no liar, and had it at first hand, and not by hearsay, when he wrote of it.

Aurea prima sata est aetas, quae vindice nullo,
sponte sua, sine lege fidem rectumque colebat.
poena metusque aberant, nec verba minantia fixo
aere legebantur, nec supplex turba timebat
iudicis ora sui, sed erant sine iudice tuti.

Would you have me continue, sir, or shall I read to you in Greek perhaps, or Hebrew, or some modern tongue? This runs trippingly even now, being one of his most favourite texts.

Does it not speak of the golden age, when all mankind did live at peace with one another? I thought so. There was a lady once, took me to Ireland as her companion, after I left my father's house. Who would laugh at my reading in such parrot fashion, and told me something of the meaning. I would I had known this when I was wont to read aloud, for then I might have had some joy of it, and so performed my task more willingly.

I see that the flies vex you. Would you have me shut the window? Things putrefying in this hot weather, I fear they are numerous. Vinegar will not drive them off, though it was put on the panes this morning. I shall never be rid of them, I think, this being an old house, and a poor neighbourhood. I will try fanning, sir, that may drive them off.

5

She was most kind to me, the lady Merian, treating me like a daughter, having promised so to do. As I never yet had been by my true parent. She did teach me, so I got a smattering of learning, which made me hunger to know more. For appetite comes from feeding. I have seen it oft amongst the little ones I teach, how they will pester me with why and wherefore, so each reply provokes yet one more question.

Girls are as much imbued with eager curiosity as are their brothers. I know this, sir, both as a woman and a mother, and from this schoolroom too. See you that verse writ neatly on the wall? The pupil who did this, her name is Mary, and had she been born John, her father wealthy, she might have made her mark upon the world, as you did, sir, or even as my father. But she must fetch and carry for her mother, help mind the shop, and find herself a husband, and lose all other thoughts in household cares.

I wish that you might see her as she is now, so fresh and eager, with an appetite for all that I can give her. And more, much more, had I the means in this poor room. But soon her mother will be scolding, she reads instead of sewing, wastes much time by writing when she should be hemming sheets or making shirts. Then will she come no more, but I will think on her, and pray she finds contentment.

My father, sir, had no need to think on aught but study, though his appetite for learning was uncommon. We had an old servant who had been with him since childhood, having worked in his parents' house when but a child herself. She it was who had to sit up late, so he would not set the house afire with burning of his candle. And I but a child myself, so she would tell us, nodding with sleep and like to tumble from my stool with weariness. I took against learning even then, she said, for I must be up at dawn to sweep hearths and fetch water.

The apple of his doting mother's eye, the great hope of his father, being the firstborn son – when did he ever fetch and carry, hew wood, or clean his boots? His father was a scrivener, but of the middling sort, who came of yeoman stock and sought to have his sons rise far above him by spending on their education.

Such zeal as my father did show, even in youth, is a rare thing indeed, and some would say against nature. So our old servant would have it, who ever after maintained it had been the ruin of his eyes. If God had meant us to read books in the night, she said, he would have made the moon to shine like the sun. She was much given to such homespun philosophy.

The many books within our house were ever the bane of her life, making but dust and clutter in small rooms, and so breeding moths and flies to plague us, and worse also. This was her opinion, to be voiced out loud at times of cleaning. She thought that long service did give her a kind of licence.

I speak of her, since she made common cause with us, and with our grumbling. In truth, sir, I found it hard, in my youth, to be roused from sleep at my father's bidding, when the Muse was on him. And though it may be thought a rare honour now, to have heard his stick knocking on the wall in the small hours and go to him with a candle to write at his dictation, I cannot say it made me fond of verse. I would rather have stayed snug in bed, and my sister also. She, being my senior by several years, had done such tasks far longer, when I could not yet read or write. Much soured by broken nights and tedious days, her tongue grew tart, so she would wish him dead upon occasion, caring little who should hear her.

My sister is long since dead. Had she lived, as I have, into riper years, I doubt not she had wished those words unspoken. In ageing, we forgive our elders, is this not so? But such words were spoken, I will not deny it, in youthful, hasty rage. That they rankled with him, the whole world knows, our quarrels being made public after his death. I am sorry for it, yet was he unkind also, in thinking not on our youth.

Genius is exigent, you say? I know this, sir, but did not know it then. I knew him but as a harsh father, who cared not for us but as we could help him, since he was blind. He was never truly young, I think, as other men are. Indeed, I have heard my uncle say that he was much misliked whilst at the university, for being too earnest. And so he cared not how it might be for us under his roof, being young, and full of youthful high spirits.

Had he thought us worthy to share his labours, and get some profit from them, we might have lived peaceably enough together, but our sex made us unworthy. I find this mighty strange, thinking, as he did, that the purpose of education should be to redeem the faults of our first parents. Must we not be saved also? And Eve, being the greater sinner, has surely more need of saving by such means? But we durst not argue. Women and servants must obey, not speak their mind.

My grandfather, being a practic, who had got some standing by thrift and industry, thought the purpose of education was to rise in the world, and so he sent his sons to school, and then to Cambridge. My father was intended for the Church, his brother for the law, both worthy estates which do a man honour. And indeed, my uncle did well enough, and died with a Sir to his name, and was much respected. But my father despised the clergy. He was fortunate in having a loving father that let him continue so long at the university, when he but pursued learning for its own sake, and not to be ordained. For this was a great expenditure of capital, and generous in a careful moneylender, such as he was, being a scrivener by trade.

Such indulgence in a father is much to be envied, I think. Seven years he studied at the university, and then was able to study the world by travelling through it. This is no mean gift for a father to give his son, but the world knows he was worthy of it. I would I had been given mere crumbs from such a rich table, if not to keep my body from want, then my soul from hunger.

Would you have me shut the casement? I can scarce hear myself speak. The fishwife has a lusty voice, but her cod stinks. She goes first to wealthy houses, and seeks to fob us off with foul remnants, that are poor. I dine mostly on bread and cheese, having so few pence to spend. It is simple fare, and but little labour.

A few crumbs of wisdom from my father's table, as I told you, sir, if it kept me not from want, women's learning being frowned upon, might yet have made me richer far in spirit. I have heard it from my uncle, that the school at St Paul's where both he and my father did go, had a tradition that no more than one hundred and fifty-three boys were to be instructed gratis, since Simon Peter drew one hundred and fifty-three fishes in the miraculous draught. But we are not fish, sir, to be fried for supper, but Christian souls, all worthy of redemption, and a father should share with his children that which he has, whether it be gold or learning.

Aptitude, sir? I know not. But I can recite you Virgil even now, though it is but foreign sounds to me, and a lifetime since I read it out loud to him. I do not wish to boast. I am no genius, but yet no fool. It is true that not all minds are alike apt for study. Having kept school I know this well enough. But the fault lies oft in the teaching, not the pupils. If a pudding finds no favour at the table, 'tis the cook we blame, not those who will not eat. And then, if I am my father's daughter in feature, as you are pleased to tell me, would it not be strange if such likeness were all on the surface, and no similitude beneath? This I know: I had no aptitude for making lace, or stitching with gold thread, and yet I was put to it. It is hard labour, and but poorly paid, and will damage eyesight as surely as reading.

I doubt that every boy who went to school with my father had equal aptitude. Indeed, my uncle, being of a free and easy nature, and much unlike my father, has confessed to me and to his children, that he would oft wish himself elsewhere when in school, and dream of ball games, flying kites, and all such sports. But gazing out the window he would read the dread words there inscribed – AUT DOCE AUT DISCE AUT DISCEDE, which, being translated, warned 'either teach, or learn, or leave', and so sent his wandering eyes back to his books.

A stern warning, sir, but I think it apt. I teach no Latin here, but my children know they must apply themselves or go to harder tasks, and tedious labour. Their parents can but ill afford the few pence they pay me and, to tell truth, there are some who have not paid, but how can I turn their little ones away? Would you do it? I have not the heart to deny them the knowledge which is mine to give. I but wish it were more.

When they leave here they must work, and work hard. There are some who spare the labour of child-ish hands but grudgingly, being poor, and without hired labour. They would have results, sir, or else their schooldays are ended. The children, knowing this, are apt to work with a will, and look upon school as like to a holiday.

You see how I must live, being a poor man's widow. It is hard to come to this, after a life of much hardship, and sorrow also. I would not take charity, could I live decently without it, and have ever tried to survive by my own industry. But those who enter the world with nothing are like to die so, for all their toil. I have found this out, in a long life amongst the humble. Though a great man's daughter, I have sunk in the world, as a daughter must, not being heir to his learning, and having no dowry to recommend me. If we cannot rise by matrimony we are like to fall, having no other way.

I was married to a decent man, ever industrious. But times were hard, and now I must fend for myself. There was no surfeit to be put by, such as my father was heir to from his father. I would not have you think me bitter, for I have long since forgiven him his harshness to me, and to my sisters. I could do no less, it being our Christian duty so to do, and besides, I have much pride in him. But if the truth must be told, he got more from his father, to help him in the world, than ever we got from him.

There's a knocking at the door - what can it be? The child who works for me is deaf, I fear, and will not go to answer. You must excuse me. I will return directly.

I cannot think who it should be at this hour. It is almost dusk. Few hawkers come so late and, besides, would call. Why, young Barnaby, what brings you here at this time – have you not had your fill of lessons? Your mother sent you, and with this? Bring it in. She is most kind.

This is young Barnaby, sir, one of my pupils, and amongst the brightest that I have coming to me. His mother keeps a shop, and sends this mutton pie, but freshly baked, for me. Will you not bow to this fine gentleman? I would not have him think I teach you no manners.

Truly, sir, I could wish his father had the means for it, to keep him at his studies, if a place could be found for him, to teach him more than I know. It grieves me to think such lively wits should not be led to higher things, but waste themselves.

He likes to read, sir, and has long since exhausted my little store of books. Can memorize a poem so speedily, word perfect, it would astonish you. And so I think he does it from love, and not from duty. And will ask such questions as I have no answer to, being but an unschooled woman, without benefit of university.

Why, he will do his sums, and learn by rote so speedily, he lacks diversion. And so he will plague me with questions – why do the stars shine? And what brings winter? What makes the rain to fall, and whence comes it? I am hard put to it, to satisfy him.

But I fear it will all go to waste, his parents being poor. Westminster will not take a mutton pie for their fees, nor St Paul's neither. Could you not use your influence, sir, to get him a place gratis? He is a good child, as well as gifted, and will repay your trouble. Think you do it for my father's sake, if not for his, the child being unknown to you. Who knows, he may be another such, and do his country service which shall last unto the end of time.

Now, Barnaby, let the gentleman hear the poem you learnt but yesterday. Do not stand abashed, for I know you can speak boldly enough. This fine gentleman knows more of poesie than you and I together, and it will please him mightily to hear one so young recite so prettily.

Come now, let us have it then. 'How doth the little busy bee' . . . He has it by heart, sir, I assure you, and the rest of Dr Watts also. I have had the children learn one poem each week, as the author recommends. It is indeed an easy way for them to imbibe great truths simply, and get some pleasure by it, as well as virtue. Come, child, what of the last verse then? Has the sun addled your brain this day? 'In books, or work, or healthful play' . . . how does it go on? 'Let my first years be past' . . . now you have it. I thought you would shame me, that are my prize pupil. It is the rhyme that sticks in the memory, though my father was much against it, and despised it so. That 'past' should rhyme with 'last' is a great help to the infant mind – you see how it tripped from his tongue with but a little prompting.

You may go, child. And thank your mother most heartily for the pie. I shall have it for my supper. And this gentleman also, if he will stay to sup with me. I am sure it will be to our liking.

He is a good child, and has quite won my heart with his diligence. Had he more schooling than I can give, he would surely profit from it. Not that I would have him so learned as my father, and the classics, I believe, are now but little thought of. Mr Clarke, my late husband, was wont to say that such learning had no uses but to make the poor think themselves more ignorant than in truth they were, and thus keep them humble. Which was why both law and Holy Writ had long been in the Latin tongue, so that the common sort might not know for themselves either truth or justice, but have it told to them by those who had been to school and university, this being a privilege of those who ruled us.

But we can all read the Bible now, and such classics as my father was wont to study, why, they are turned into English, so our fine young ladies, that now have so much leisure, may read them. And in rhyming couplets too, to ease the task. No, sir, there is more to be got from school than Latin grammar, and the child must earn a livelihood, when all is said and done.

Will you take supper with me, sir? His mother bakes a fine pie, and there is a little ale in the scullery, to keep it cool. I know it is but humble fare, but I think you will find the pie to your liking. She does a good trade, and works hard, his father being often without work, as much from vagaries of fashion and demand, as from uncertain health. I know how it is, being a weaver's widow. I have seen her weep, not for herself, being weary, but for her children, born to a world which holds nothing for them but fruitless toil, and little hope of better things to come.

To send her child to me, it is an act of faith. And it costs her dear, in losing of his labour. I fear, being quite untaught, illiterate, she thinks too highly of me, of the learning I can give him. This is a grief to me, sir, I confess it. I can scarce look in her eyes, for the hope I see in them. A kind of pleading, like unto a prayer, that I would not betray. You know the look a favourite dog will give you, his head upon your knee? She has that air about her when she brings her boy, or comes to fetch him, and asks me how he does. I tell her, truthfully, he is a clever child, and she looks proud, and smiles, and seems less weary, and thanks me from her heart.

She has little enough to thank me for, did she but know it. If none will help him he must be self-taught, for that which I can teach him will not do, when all is said and done. I think there is a rumour in this neighbourhood, and his mother heard it, that my father was a famous man, the most learned in all Christendom! I would he had made me his heir, though but a woman, not for myself, having no wish to be mocked as a learned lady, but to fulfil their expectation, and feed their children's minds, so their bellies be full in after years.

I think on this now, sir, that did not think on it in my youth. How should our children learn, if their mothers cannot read? For we must all be mothers, and help our children prosper in the world. I would not have any son of mine made stupid by too much learning. I beg your pardon, sir, I mean no offence. But, more than the rudiments of reading and arithmetic, this can be a source of both pleasure and profit in later life, and so should be taught more widely, not merely to the rich.

And so, sir, I would have you think on young Barnaby, using your good offices in his favour. It would give me much joy, and his mother also. You are leaving, sir, and will not partake of the pie? I think the coffee house beckons, with more amusing fare than I can offer. No, no, I am not offended. I take it kindly that gentlemen from the great world should think fit to call on me.

TWO

THINK YOU I never quarrelled with your father whilst he lived, or thought to go from him, our dispute being yet fresh? Come, child, this is mere foolishness, and well you know it. As we make our bed, so we must lie, and many a woman has greater cause to rue her wedding day than ever you have had. Come, sit by me, and wipe your eyes. I fear you should be abed, and that's the cause of it. No woman in my day would get up so soon. You have told me oft enough there is no help for it, but we should manage well enough a few days more. Think you I came to live under your roof to be a burden merely? I will do what I can, as long as may be.

It is your grief that speaks, else you would not take on so for a trifle. I know this, having lost so many babes in my time. A woman's humour is strange enough at these times, but when the cause is lost, and buried in the churchyard, it can unhinge us quite. I know whereof I speak, daughter, and so, by now, should you, being no stranger to such grief.

Your hands are cold, my dear, and I like not your pallor. Could we not have a fire in this room? The price of coal is high this winter, but I fear for you. Mr Foster would not begrudge it, since you are but lately risen from childbed. Do not protest, I know him to be tender of your welfare, and we can be sparing of other things. I will go cold to bed, and supperless too, if need be. It matters little to me, being old. And perhaps there will be more work this winter. Your brother seems sure of it.

I hope it may be so, else he will be lodging here, unwed, for all his life. I would see him with a good wife before I die, to be a comfort to him. I think the Widow Cutler looks kindly on him, and has her own shop, and lodgings with it, but she is old, and would bear him no children. What think you? That wedlock is no comfort, and a snare?

Come, child, what else would you have in this life? You are peevish, else you would not speak so. Mr Foster is a good man, though he has his faults, as all men do. In marriage we must endeavour to love a man for his defects, it being easy enough to be fond of his virtues. You smile, daughter, and I am right glad of it. Let us have no more speaking of divorce in this family, for it has brought scandal enough, and besmirched my father's name. Besides, divorcing is but for men, and an adulterer's charter, a woman being without independent means. And so she would end a burden on the parish, like any poor soul with child and out of wedlock.

But I hear a knocking at the door. Sit still, and I will answer. I think it must be the professor come to call, from Gresham College. What hour is it? I had quite forgot the time. Is my cap set neatly? It must be him, for his servant carries books, no doubt to try me, stamping his feet from cold. His face quite red with it, and the breath rising from them like steam from a kettle. I am coming, sir.

And no fire neither. I beg your pardon, sir. We keep the hearth unlit during daylight hours, the price of coals being so high. This is my daughter,

Mrs Foster. If you will send your servant to the kitchen, she will see he gets something to warm him.

Oh no, sir, I do not complain. The public has been very generous in coming to my assistance. I would I might even now live by my own industry. Until lately I kept a school at Moorfields, but now my eyesight begins to fail. I am fortunate to have a child yet living, though I would not be a burden to her. She is not well, having but lately risen from childbed, but there is no speaking to her, she will not rest as she should.

I see you have brought books to try me. Greek is it, or Latin? Though my eyes grow dim, I can recite you long passages without looking at the page, having read them out loud so frequently. Would you have Ovid, or Virgil? *Arma virumque cano*, and so forth. There was a gentleman came but lately, did try me on Euripides. I think he could scarce credit what he heard, his eyes as wide as though I had been an automaton, and not a living woman. And so I was, if the truth be told, being used as such, but for my eyes. I know not what I read, and recite but parrot fashion.

Elizabeth, is the servant thawed out in the kitchen? Think on it, the professor has been to Nantwich, and seen my stepmother! She must be a great age now, surely, for she was no spring chicken when she wed my father, being all of twenty-four years old, and hard put to it to find a husband, had he not been blind. No, sir, there has been no correspondence between us for many years, there being so little liking when my father lived. For she was a very termagant, and I had nothing from her but scolding.

To think she yet lives. And has she all her faculties

still? I warrant her tongue is as sharp as ever, if she can wag it. She must be wellnigh eighty years old, nay, more, for I was ten when she married my father, and now I am well past my allotted span of three score and ten. They do say nuns live to a great age, and she never bore children. He had more need of a housekeeper than aught else, I think, when he took her to wife. For the price of loving is oft an early death, and both my mother and his second wife did die in childbed.

It was told me some years past that she is now become God-fearing, and a pillar of the Baptist ministry. I am glad of it, for her soul's sake. For if she would see my father in the next life, she has much need of penitence in this. Such double dealing, and a forked tongue, giving him honeyed words and us but vinegar. I have heard she is become a woman of property, from what my father left her. But still the miser, and lives so frugally, the neighbours speak of Mrs Milton's feast, meaning enough but no more. Well, she has feathered her nest, that being her purpose. That like a cuckoo sought to push us out, though not yet hatched and fledged.

It is a shrewd woman marries an old man, with no appetite but for tasty stews and apple pie. I never said she was not shrewd, though a shrew with it. She knew what she was about, when her cousin put her in the way of it. He was doctor to my father, and much in his confidence. And if she would tame us, being thought unruly, she had done better to have sought to do it by loving kindness, and not harsh words.

Pardon me for speaking thus. Christian duty bids us honour our father and mother, and, though I have long since forgiven my dear father for his harshness, she was not my mother. Had she sought to be such, I would have loved her. For truly, I had need of it.

My mother died bringing me into the world, and so I never knew her. It is a hard thing to be thus deprived. A child, being young, must needs have a parent who loves it for itself, a father being remote and stern, loving us rather for our virtues. And I think our father did mislike us, not for our lack of them, but for being our mother's daughters, and this we could not mend.

I would not speak of this, sir, for it pains me. Though I did not know her, she bore me in her womb, and I do not believe her to have been a sinful woman. Foolish perhaps, and worthy of our pity, but no more. She gave her life for mine, and for this I honour her and love her in my heart. Would I might have loved her in her life, I might have looked back to my youth with happier heart, and fonder memories. I honour my father, for he did great things in the world. But no man yet died giving birth to his child, and for this I must love her, for all her frailty.

Daughter, I would not have you think I deem it right that a young wife should leave her husband after but a few weeks of wedlock, visiting her parents, and refusing to return when sent for. She knows whereof I speak, sir, it is between us. I believe matrimony to be a sacred bond, and hope my children will ever think likewise. We are decent people, who live decently, and know our duty. But those were turbulent times, a civil war beginning, and travel hazardous. I have heard my grandam say the roads were perilous betwixt Forest Hill and London, so she and Mr Powell would not have their daughter set forth.

There are two sides to every coin, sir, and the fault was not all with my mother. Though I know it is a wife's duty to obey her husband, she but obeyed her father in marrying a man she scarcely knew, except her father, being in his debt, would have him for his son-in-law to buy him off. So now she but obeyed in failing to return to one thought renegade, and like to lose his head, the war once won.

Besides, I have heard my grandam say her daughter was sent away, my father not liking her conversation, and thinking he had made an ill bargain, the dowry being unpaid, and the girl having nothing but foolishness in her young head, which had captured him with fresh looks and youthful prettiness. And so he thought her an unfit companion for his gravity and serious ambition.

You find some credence in this version of the event, having studied his pamphlets on divorce? I am glad to hear it, sir, for I think my poor mother has been much maligned in this regard. I have ever found it strange, that he should think a meet and happy conversation to be the chief end of matrimony, and yet deny girl children equal education with their brothers. Surely it is a foolish hope that we should converse wisely, if we are kept ignorant? Besides, had he no chance to talk with her before he was betrothed, and so find out if they were like to suit? He married in haste, sir. Indeed, we know this to be so, for he rode out a bachelor to collect a debt, and rode back wedded, a thing not be expected in a man of older years and studious habits, and left his kin astounded.

My father was wont to put upon others a frailty he would not own. I have seen this in him, and have ever thought it his chiefest fault. I must speak frankly, sir. You have not come to the poor streets of Spitalfields to hear me utter falsehoods. If he chose his bride unwisely, was this her fault? He was twice her age and, as the world judges, he had twice her wisdom, and so I think him doubly culpable for any error. He knew this, sir, and so his loathing for her was but doubled.

If he did marry in haste, he had much leisure to repent, they being parted till the war was wellnigh ended. But though many do repent them, they are not minded to write pamphlets on divorce, and so bring scandal on their heads. It is not Christian, sir, and though he might twist and turn the Bible to his ends, and say it meant by this some other thing, being ill translated or interpreted, it would not do. If he was vilified for writing so, I think, sir, he did bring it on himself, for seeking to use women like discarded garments, to be thrown out at pleasure.

The shock nigh killed me – thus my grandam. She was no reading woman but, the scandal being so great, reports of it had reached the countryside. The minister spoke against it in church, to our eternal shame, as she recalled it. My poor dear daughter, so I told your mother, God rest her blessed soul, first throws you out of doors, and now would cast you off entirely, leaving you quite dishonoured, neither maid nor widow nor an honourable wife. For what man will look upon another's leavings, and not despise it? I fear this law which he would have to favour lawless men, licentious libertines, now that these godless rene-gades have won the war, may yet find favour.

So she advised my hapless mother, who was wont to obey her parents in all things. Though a wife in name, she was yet a child, and childlike. I had this also from our old servant, who was fond of her, and thought her hardly used. She would speak of her as chattering like a magpie, gay as a country thrush that sang about her work, until she heard her master coming out the study, or his voice upon the stair, when she would blench and fall silent. As though she had forgot her married state and liked not to remember, fearing his harshness and authority.

Though I knew her not, I think I know her as I do myself, for I was much in the same case as his daughter. And she might have been his daughter, being so young. You can have no notion, Elizabeth, how it is to live in such a house. Mr Clarke, my late husband and her father, was also my senior by many years but, being no scholar and a simple man, a mere mechanical, a weaver like my son and son-in-law, did not think himself my better, and despised not my understanding. What he read, I could read also, and all things were freely discussed between us. You think yourself ill used upon occasion, daughter, but it is much the same betwixt you and Mr Foster. Though you may disagree from time to time, you have your say, and say it loudly, and after make it up and are friends once more. Think yourself fortunate, and make your peace with him.

I beg your pardon, sir, we speak of private matters. I know it is now the custom that women of the better sort should have some cultivation, to make them fit companions for their husbands, and able to converse in drawing rooms. It was not so in my youth, nor in my mother's time. We were bred for household tasks, hard labour and child-bearing. And if we could read it was but to know our Bible.

I have some pity for my mother's case, whatever the truth of it. She knew her duty, but being so long a daughter and but newly wedded, she was accustomed rather to obey her parents than her husband. And it is a hard thing to be married to a creditor who comes knocking at the door, so as to fob him off. Like so much chattel. I had no dowry, sir, and married a poor man, but I ever knew he took me for myself.

And so, being married on account of an old debt, she incurred but a new and greater in the marrying, her dowry being unpaid. He never forgave it, sir, and oft did speak of it. Let them have their mother's dowry, so he would say in his last years, we being her daughters, and as much unloved, and all the rest to Betty. And so he kept her sweet, his dearest Betty, who pandered to his whims, so she might be a widow who lived at ease. As she now does.

Sir, you are cold. The fire must be lit, I think. Besides, it grows dark, and it will spare us a candle. The night draws in so fast. We shall have snow before morning, the clouds hanging so low. This early dusk speaks of it. I would not have you deem us inhospitable, though we are poor. I am cold myself, and I see how you rub your fingers.

Do not fret, Elizabeth. You are not yet well. I will not have you penny-pinching, and catch your death from it. She is married to a good man, sir, who is as anxious in her behalf as I am. But work has been hard to get this winter, and ill paid. The rent must be found, and so he will preach thrift and stern accounting more than needful. To fall sick from parsimony is no good housekeeping, and I think he would not bury his wife for a few coals.

Had he ridden out himself to fetch her from Forest Hill, it might have been otherwise. I speak now of my father. For if there was some vexation between them, she leaving London so soon after their marriage, and being not back at Michaelmas as promised, she must have thought it high-handed in him to send a messenger to fetch her home, and not ride out himself. Such feeling as she might have had for him, if not quite nipped in the bud by earlier coldness, must now have been extinguished. Is it any wonder her parents sent his messenger away, and did it curtly? Is this the way to woo an errant wife, if so she was? And if the previous fault was all upon his side, as my grandmother would ever have it, he but compounded it.

Though a wife be got much like a mare at market, yet must she be wooed for easy riding, with coaxing and tender words. And I doubt not my grandfather, thinking at the first to have disarmed his creditor by making him a son-in-law, had changed his mind since then, the war once started and my father being of the opposing faction. Why, had the king been victorious, as they both thought and hoped, their daughter had been but a youthful widow to the gallows. Had they been star-crossed lovers, and as much besotted as Romeo and Juliet, their path had not been easy. And my father was no Romeo. They were, as our old servant would have it, as ill-paired as ox and mare in one yoke.

And yet, sir, as we make our bed, so we must lie. I fear my father, though old in years when he married, was but a virgin in the ways of the world, having seen but little of it, his eyes being ever on ancient texts, and he scarce leaving his study. As my uncle would have it, my father was as like to see the promised dowry of a thousand pounds, and the loan with interest added, for which he first rode out to Oxfordshire, as he was to see the sun rise in the west and gold coins grow on trees. For the Powells' estate had long since been mortgaged to the hilt, from easy living and careless ways, and such a man will promise his bed for the morrow so he can but sleep easy tonight.

A like foolishness, coming from too much study, beguiled him when he took my mother to wife so hastily. As you say, he hints of it in writing of divorce – can you recall the words? I would have my daughter hear them. Who have spent their youth chastely, haste too eagerly to light the nuptial torch? And much in the same wise? I have heard him speak so in later years, how bestial necessity will make a man blind, till he wake to bondage with an unfit wife. Indeed, I have heard him say he was glad he had lost his eyes when he took his dear Katharine to wife, since, not being ensnared by her looks, he heard but her conversation and so chose wisely. And though he would not have a young man sow wild oats, this being contrary to virtue, it were better he went to the stews than to find himself chained to a stinking carcass in the marriage bed.

I blush to speak so, sir, but my father did not mince his words upon occasion, as you must know, having read his works. His hate being aroused, he could find more common words of loathing, more abuse, than is thought fit in genteel society, and was not shy to use them. I have been the target, and know whereof I speak. All those not of his opinion, the lower sort, unschooled and ignorant, and females also, great ladies excepted, could rouse his scorn. Like Jove from up on high he cast his thunder on a despised rabble down below. This was the price of his sublimity, as this age now calls it.

Ideals can make us harsh, is it not so? We have all had dreams when young, and had to wake to the real world, and make our peace with it as best we could. So I tell my daughter here, when she is troubled. None had dreams more fanciful, more glowing, than my father. I think you know this, sir, being familiar with his poetry. Yet none had lived as little in the common world, being bookish in his habits. It made him cruel to such lesser mortals as lived in it, and disappointed him. I know this, having been the object of his sarcasm.

Well, there is more to marriage than four bare legs in the bed, as our old servant was wont to warn us in our youth. My sister Mary being apt to speak of wedlock as the means whereby she would escape from out our father's house, and from his tyranny. For my poor sister, bearing our mother's name, and most like to her in feature, was most his enemy, and early grew rebellious. She was oft abused for being too like our mother, having her defects of nature, so he said, and a pert and ready tongue. Such words but made her more unruly. She said she would sooner be like our mother, who was loving and kind, as she remembered her, than like unto her father, being neither. And so their war continued.

It is a hard thing, when the sins of our parents are visited upon us. He had no liking for us, for our mother's sake, though we had no part in the choosing. It was you chose my mother, not I, so my sister would retort. Taking dictation at his behest had given her some edge of learning, despite her sex, and his contempt. God gave us free will, you tell us, to choose for better or for worse, and if you chose for worse, then more fool you. I am not to blame, for Christ died on the Cross so that the sins of the fathers, aye, and of our mothers, first and last, should not be visited upon us. And so I stand absolved.

She had been wiser to have held her tongue, for there was too much truth in her words not to rankle, and to think himself in error was not to my father's liking. Children and fools tell the truth, lacking the wisdom to stay silent before those who rule them. A silent cunning had served her better, and to call him fool was but blowing on the coals so the sparks flew in her face.

And then there was no end to hearing of my mother's unpaid dowry, as though we had been to blame in this likewise. They shall have their mother's dowry, he would say, the rest going to Betty. I doubt not my mother heard him speak of it also, this being her father's default. For such debts as Mr Powell had had before the war were now made desperate, the king's side losing. I have heard my grandam speak of this time, how all was lost, their property being sequestrated. I never thought to live to see the day, she'd say, the shame of it! For the remembrance of it much distressed her in old age. And all for being on the side of rightful monarchy! My husband in poor health, and eleven sons and daughters in the house who must be fed and clothed, the sons made gentlemen, the daughters married! If I have got grey hairs I got them then – for she would boast about her looks when young, how many courted her before she married Mr Powell.

So it was, the Powell fortunes being at their lowest ebb, my father and his bride were reconciled. My grandam would tell us of it with tears in her eyes, though smiling also. Tears for her daughter, long since laid to rest, smiles for us, her offspring, of whom she was most fond. The old, I think, are thus. Dwell in the past and weep for it too readily. I feel it in myself.

As she told it – Mary, so I spoke to your dear mother, we must get us to London. You must fall upon your knees and beg his pardon. I care not whose fault it was, or who spoke first in anger, this is no time for niceties. The war is lost, and we are ruined utterly. I never thought our state would come to this, but it is so. You are Mrs Milton, and must take your rightful place within his home. I have four other daughters who must be got husbands, and you have one already. He loved you once, and will do so again, if you are sweet with him, and do his bidding. I fear we must act speedily, else, being in the victor's camp, his notions on divorce may be made law, and then you are undone. Who will have you then, being cast off by him? It will not help you, the fault being his, or not, it is all one. Being damaged goods, you may sing heigh-ho for a husband.

We must all live in the real world at last, for all our dreams. Is it not so, daughter? Men and women both must do so, if they would live together, and be a help unto each other. I think my mother, in the years between, had grown from scarce more than a child into a woman, and so more sensible. She did her parents' bidding, surprised my father in a neighbour's house, where he was wont to call, and fell upon her knees.

She sought forgiveness, sir, from dire necessity, and he forgave her, as a Christian should. I know not who was most to blame for their parting, but I think my father, being he who forgave, the righteous victor in this civil war, ignored such errors as must fall to him, and so he made her suffer. Her life with him was but one long repentance. I have heard our servant call it so, and I believe her.

To forgive is not enough. He should have loved

her, sir, and raised her up, for to do less is not forgiveness but a mere semblance of it. And so it proved in the event, he despising us for her remembered faults. A woman's lot in wedlock is not easy. I know this, having brought ten children into the world, and losing seven in infancy. But Mr Clarke was ever tender of me, and sought my welfare as he sought his own. My daughter here must say the same of Mr Foster. But my mother, sir, she had but condonation from her husband, and little else. Seven years of wedlock followed from their re-uniting, she dying at my birth, the fourth childbed she endured.

I have much pity for her. For childhood has an end, and we escape from out our father's house into the world, and look to this in youth. But wedlock has no end except in death, and this most likely, being brought to bed. And, though we pray to God in such extremity, it is our husband's fondness gives us comfort here below, our time drawing nigh. It is a deed of love that we must do, in much pain and fear. But where such love is lacking, to lift us up, then 'tis scarce to be endured.

Where are you going, daughter? I will not have you catch your death out of doors. I think, sir, it distresses her to hear us speak of childbed, being scarce out of it, and the child not living. I wish I might have bit off my tongue, rather than speak so. She should be in her bed, but will not rest, seeking rather to find distraction in going about her work. You saw her pallor. Grief has her in its grip. She has wept much this past month, and refused nourishment. I would I knew how to counsel her and give her comfort, but her ears are sealed at present and will not hear. Say too much, and she will but quarrel with those nearest to her.

Is it snowing? I have seen her venture out of doors this past week, and it so cold. I think we shall have snow before nightfall. The clouds look as though they would touch the rooftops. She should be in her bed. Though poor, we are not yet so poor that it should come to this. Did you know, my eldest sister died in childbed likewise, as did our mother? Though born a cripple she yet found a husband, for she was beautiful, a gentle soul who never gainsaid any man. Being defective in her speech, and not able to read aloud with fluency, for she would stammer, she was spared my father's rigours. And she never learnt to write. But I fear she was not apt for wedlock either, her body being infirm. And so her first child brought her to her death, and was buried with her.

It grieved me much to hear of it. I lived in Ireland then, with Mr Clarke. I think, sir, such a loss is doubly felt when we are far off. I have but lately lost my other son, Caleb, who went to live in India many years since. I wish I might have seen him once more, before he died, and spoken with him. But I have seen his son, young Abraham, who came to England from Madras but a few years ago. He looked so like his father when he left these shores, so youthful, strong, and upright in his bearing, I thought that time had played a trick on me, and here he stood, my Caleb, as he was when last I saw him, on the verge of manhood. Though he bears my husband's name – for Mr Clarke was christened Abraham – I saw in him my Caleb come again. He had his eyes, his features, though a little less in height. I wellnigh wept for joy on seeing him. Being well-mannered, he was respectful, but yet I was a stranger to him, though he was not to me, or so I fancied. Doubtless he thought me strange, to be so fond.

Alas, sir, I was deceived, since vanished time can never come again. For it was while young Abraham was here in England, the poor boy heard his father was deceased, and so he must return immediately. But though I mourned for him, I took some comfort in his son, being so like him. Caleb is dead, but something of him yet lives on.

The looms will soon be idle. The work is too poorly paid, this winter, to continue by candlelight. Urban will be back directly, now the light is going. He is a weaver also, and lodges with us here, working elsewhere in Spitalfields, in a French workshop. Such fine silks they weave, their finishings a wonder, yet are many reduced to penury, and find it hard as we do. He is now my sole surviving son, but in good health. I would he might marry before I die, and his wife bear him a son with his features. It would give me joy. But I think he will not.

He has a little of my father in him. About the eyebrows and the forehead. You will see it, if he comes. I fear he is not a reading man, for Mr Clarke put him to work at ten years old. He reads but little, and never willingly. And yet, I think, he most nearly resembles him.

Would you not say so, daughter? That Urban has some look about him of my father? I know you never knew him, but you have seen his portrait. True, he resembles me in feature, more than you do. She is like her father. Mr Addison was pleased to say: Madam, you need no other voucher – your face is a sufficient testimonial whose daughter you are. He was most kind, and was most active in my behalf until his death. It grieved me much to hear of it.

You are leaving us, sir? Will you not wait for my son? But you may see him as you walk down Pelham Street, fair-haired and small of build. Perhaps you are wise to leave before nightfall, for there are pickpockets hereabouts, and ruffians prowl the streets. I trust your servant is a brave fellow. But I see you are armed. You do well to go so, the streets being not safe for decent people now. Do not forget your books.

THREE

How quickly it grows dark, and the mending still undone. But I would not shame us by having him see our poor bits and tatters, such a fine gentleman. Did you not think him a fine gentleman? Saw you his buttons? I never saw such in all my life, and he but a commoner, and come from trade, so I surmise. But folk are grown so fine these days, and think it no sin to wear silk and lace a-plenty, and their wives know nothing of patching and mending, but are idle the whole day long, and must have a maid to dress them.

Such wealth, where it comes from I know not, but I would a little might come to those who must labour all the hours God sends, and yet find little comfort. Saw you his buttons? I think the cost would keep us all in good wool cloth this winter. And yet he was courteous, for all his finery, and sought to turn a blind eye to the poor rooms in which we live. Did you remark it, when he left the house, how his eye scarce lingered long enough to take in walls or floor, or rotten plaster? Such is the nature of civility, that would have us all one before God.

What's that you say? You would rather he saw truly, for turning a blind eye will not mend matters? What should he do, daughter, become a martyr to philanthropy? Or cease to walk abroad, for fear of seeing what he cannot mend? Besides, he came not empty-handed, as you will see if you do look upon the mantel, or so I think. He would not have me see him put the money thither, yet I saw well enough. But I can play the lady likewise, having been brought up civilly, and so played his little game as he would have me play it, affecting to see nothing.

How much is it – five whole guineas? You see, I have done better with my clacking tongue than Mr Foster at his clacking loom this day. Do not weep, daughter. 'Tis weariness that weeps in you, and I but spoke in jest. Were it not for my father, I could no more earn such wealth by idle chatter than pluck the sun from out the sky to give you warmth. You know this well enough. 'Tis my father they honour thus, and shame, such as they feel at my distress, is only as his daughter. Else they would let me languish.

Five whole guineas! Now we have money, you must get more help. I insist upon it. For you are up too soon, and so your health will suffer. Do not argue with me, I know whereof I speak. The servant you have now will not suffice. Why, she is but half a servant, being so young. Though she does what she can, poor thing, and costs but little.

And then you must have good nourishment to cheer your spirits. What would you say to a fat capon, and some Lisbon wine? Melancholy after childbirth is a fearful thing, and you are very low. Look up, daughter, and dry your eyes. Though you have lost this babe, you yet have little Liza, to be a comfort to you. I know how it is, my dear – have I not buried seven in infancy? But yet we must trust in the Lord, believing in Him. In sorrow shalt thou bring forth children, so the good Book says, and truly, it is so.

Would I were a man, that labours mightily to bring forth verses in the comfort of his study, without the spilling of a little drop of blood, and pangs but of the spirit! So they grow old, and prosper. Men may seek to change the world, but change not this, and we must suffer it as best we may.

He will come again, he says, and bring another such gentleman, who would hear me speak of bygone times. So we shall have coals this winter. Why, it begins to snow in earnest, did I not say it would? And Urban not yet home. Have no fear, daughter, we shall eat this winter, though the work is scarce, and but poorly paid. Such visitors continuing, it will save us from destitution. And though I would rather some other way could be found to keep us from want, beggars cannot be choosers, and we must be thankful for such charity.

He said I looked much like him. Poor father, it would not please him to hear it. My face has been my fortune, more so now than in my youth. What a topsyturvy world it is, to be sure, that I should earn sovereigns with my wrinkles and white hair! I see you smile at last, and I am glad of it. We must all laugh a little at how the world goes, for crying will not mend it. And thank your stars I am my father's daughter, else might we starve and no one care a jot. As many do this night, born as they were of Master Nobody or common Jack.

To be sure, child, I would rather live out my days in comfort by my own industry. Who would not, pray? I have said as much, in begging for support. Yet what profits it to fulminate in such a manner? You may spare your breath, it will change nothing. We must be thankful for their notice, that they come with their notebooks to question me, till I scarce know if I be in this age or the last. Pride is a luxury for those that can afford shoe leather, and fine buttons to their coats. Such work as we do with our hands, though skilled, will not spare us the humiliation of begging when we are old.

I fear 'tis so, daughter, though you work all the hours God sends, and your little one also, once she is old enough to wind spools and help in the shop. I fear 'tis so, for all our proud talk of making our own way, and thrift and industry. Have I not heard your father speak thus, in our early days? And yet his widow has but a widow's mite. We would be master of our own workshop, thinking thereby to rule our fate, to sink or swim as we be prudent or profligate, work hard or lie abed. But there are forces quite beyond our knowing, to wreck the humblest hopes, like gales and storms at sea which blow small skiffs to shipwreck. I have seen it in my time, child, and know whereof I speak. Your father was no idler, nor I neither, and yet we left you nothing but a poor widow, to sit a burden at your hearth. For which I am right sorry.

So, she lives at Nantwich yet, and is prosperous. That is the way to widowhood. Marry an old man and keep his goods, not bury seven infants in the graveyard. There is but little profit to be got from that, and you survive. Forgive me, daughter. It slipped from me, I know not why. I did not mean to pain you by speaking of such matters. But she is living proof, if proof were needed, that 'tis a lie, that industry and thrift go well rewarded and idleness does not. We are but a nation of hypocrites, I fear, to have thought thus. We were misled, that thought so in my youth – that we are free to rise and free to fall, and need not charity, but only virtue.

It is not so. Those who have a modicum of comfort think themselves virtuous, that are but fortunate, and should thank God for it, and show a little pity for their neighbours that are not so. And yet they hold themselves accountable for their good fortune, and others for the misery they suffer. I fear it is so, daughter. I have heard sermons enough in my time, both in the chapel and out of it.

Had we gone to the New World and not to Ireland, who knows, it might have been another story. They say the life is hard, yet do many prosper there. But for the troubles in King James's time, we had lived out our days in some comfort. And then the Frenchmen come to take our business, and watered silk suddenly all the fashion, so plain silk would not do. Who could have foretold such sudden dislocations? We think ourselves free, and take much pride in owning our own loom, or even two, in being a small master rather than a servant, and yet we are the slaves of chance and fashion. The factor takes the fat, and leaves but little lean for us to thrive on. We but labour for him, when all is said and done. He farms out work and takes the richest harvest.

So much for independence, child. I have had my fill of it, these fifty years. The market is a jungle, and beasts of prey do flourish there. The honest man goes under, like as not.

Five whole guineas! And all for a little gossip. You shall have a wool cloak, daughter, and new shoes to wear on Sunday. And I would have you light a candle to mend by, to spare your eyes. For none will pay such as us when we have lost our sight. You see how it is with me, else I might be teaching school even now. For he would have me up at all hours of the day and night. Dark or light, 'twas all one to him, having no sight. And ever had been, so our old servant said, which was the ruin of his eyes in earlier years. Mine too, I think, for I have had to wear spectacles since eighteen years of age, and from what other cause, I know not.

Such a fine gentleman! Though he use his eyes, he will do so to some purpose, and so he walks abroad with silver buckles on his shoes, and when he reads 'tis not by rushlight, nay, nor tallow neither. I have seen how it is, daughter, those who have thoughts in their heads, and have been to the university, and can read in ancient books and know whereof they read, the world sees them well fed. They do not walk the streets, crying 'for charity'.

Did you not see how easily he parted with his coin just now? And all for a little learning, for going to school, and afterwards to college. 'Tis an investment, like any other, and brings more dividends than buying of a loom will ever do. My grandfather knew what he did, in sending of his sons to Cambridge. For he was but of humble stock, you know, his father being a yeoman. As for stitching and making lace, as I was taught to do, to have me out of doors, 'tis but a certain path to poverty, and industry will not help us. For doing more is doing it for less, as like as not, for what is plentiful is cheap, and there are many willing hands, with starving bellies, who would do the work, and fewer wealthy ladies who will buy.

Let us throw this stocking out, daughter. Why, it is more full of holes than a colander. It will do for a dishclout, but it is not worth the mending. You must have new stockings, if there are more in such a parlous state. Thread this needle for me, for the eye escapes me, and I will do Urban's shirt. Still not home, and the snow falling so thickly, the window is nigh on obscured. Perhaps the Frenchman has more work this night, and keeps him longer. Or he has gone to call upon the widow. What think you?

I hope it is work that keeps him. Besides, I think her too old for him. That he is not such a great catch, I know this, daughter. But she might do worse, I think, being past thirty. Such women, having the means, are apt to look kindly on a youthful bachelor, poverty being of less account in their eyes.

I wish he might have had more schooling in his youth, and so gone further. You say he has no aptitude for scholarship. Think you the sons of gentlemen have aptitude? Why, they must have Latin whipped into them, and most would rather be elsewhere. And then, if he had got the taste for it in youth, he might have grown more studious.

But there, child, what's the use to think on it? If wishes were horses, beggars would ride. We must be thankful for the little we have, not ask for more. You would have more? Alas, daughter, have you not heard your father speak of this? I know he is dead long since, and you but young, and yet he spoke of it so often, how his hopes were dashed, I thought you would have some recollection of it.

He grew up a weaver's son, but with hope of better times to come, and justice here on earth. You must have heard him speak of it. How, when he was a boy, it was customary to gather round the fire on certain nights of the year, singing and playing instruments, to await His coming, and not be caught in slumber when Christ did come again. Having heard sundry prophecies, that all which had been foretold in the Book of Daniel should soon come to pass. Four beasts, he said, four empires had risen and fallen in the course of time, and now the fifth was come, the kingdom given to the saints forever. This being so, he verily believed, justice must reign, the lowlier sort must prosper like their betters, being better only through Adam's sin in Paradise. For some are rich, some poor, not by God's design but as a punishment for eating of the apple, consequent upon our first parents' crime. So now redemption comes, by time and Christ together.

This was their hope, I heard him speak of it in after years, though bitterly. We were betrayed, he said, our leaders, that did call themselves the saints, were but frail men, with all men's frailties. And yet the Book of Daniel, he believed it still, its Christian message. Four beasts, he said, four empires risen and fallen in the course of time, Babylon, Assyria, Greece and Rome. Likewise the Book of Revelation did describe the slaying of the Beast, foul Papacy, and coming in of saints.

Alas, men are but men withal, and prone to err. You think, because you are young, that you can put the world to rights, had you but the means to do it. But your father in his time, and I in my first youth, saw the world turned topsyturvy, and yet no better for it. Why, my father, at the very hub of it, these great events, who thought it right the king should lose his head, yet was like a king within his household, nay, your aunt would have it, more like to a tyrant. Despised us for our sex, and used his manservant most shabbily, so he did leave his service. I fear that property or privilege will ever rule, and so the poor, and women most of all, have naught to hope for from such overturning, and much to dread. Why, I have seen it for myself, child. Men such as my father, who would have those set above them not their betters, would keep those born below them still inferior, to do their will. To feed their purpose, not our bellies, this is their intent. And so it is that men cry liberty, to which we must submit, slavish to their authority.

You have heard me speak, I think, of the lady Merian, she who took me to Ireland as her companion. She it was who spoke her mind upon such issues, and in such a manner as I had never heard before. I fear my father, had he heard her give of her opinions, would not have thought her a fit person to have the care of me, if he had thought at all in my behalf, or cared by then what did become of me, which he did not. I can speak thus, child, she told me, for no man holds the purse strings over me, which is a rare thing indeed. I only speak as many would, if they were free to do so. Necessity doth put a brank upon our tongues, and many think that which they durst not say. So men do fear the axe, or to be thrown in jail for what they speak out loud. But what can we do, that have a censor at our pillow night and day, and hearth and house a prison of our thoughts, if we would live at ease? A sorry tale, she called it, the late history of overturning. I fear, she said, a partial vision doth affect those who would see most clearly, and trump their views out to the world, of mighty reformation, that cry liberty, liberty, yet keep their household slaves.

But 'twill not be forever thus, she said, for thoughts will out, and a door half opened can be opened wide, by those who follow after. It is ever thus, so she was wont to say, that some would ope the door for their own liberty, but slam it shut before the rest can follow. I am born free, they say, but thou, being born to serve me, that is, born a woman, are not so. Or poor, unprivileged, or what you will.

'Tis for such sophistry they'd keep us out of school, so she would tell me, on the long voyage out to Ireland. Being voluble of her opinions, I think she had need of a companion to hear her thoughts, more than to serve her. For they can argue till the cows come home, having their texts to prove them in the right, and cite at every turn. So your father, to be shot of an unfit wife, could write his pamphlets, quoting sundry texts such as an untutored girl had never heard of, that could scarce write her name. What kind of equity is this, she'd argue, when some are ever in the wrong, not from having sinned, but lack of knowledge to defend themselves, being disbarred from pleading?

'Tis property that rules the world, not justice. So she would say. And we are but as chattel. For those who fought and won, if for a while, during the late troubles, fought but for property and not for justice, else had they been levellers all.

She spoke most frankly, early widowhood making her free to speak so, and gold the oil to her tongue. Each cares but for his own interest, so she said. So it was in the late wars, and this was their undoing. He who is without property hath no interest in the kingdom, if he do merely breathe, so said the men of property who led the fight, and so said Cromwell. So merchants said, merchants must have their rights, but not apprentices. Apprentices, meanwhile, would give unto themselves some say, but not to beggars. And as for women, they came last of all, being but sinful daughters of Eve, mother to all our woes. Or so they tell us, they who would not hold themselves culpable for their own ills.

So each sort had their faction, and few could see

beyond their noses, or find a common purpose. 'Tis a rare master gives his servant leave to speak, and the husband that would hear his wife truly speak her mind is not yet born, I think. So fathers rule their children, men their wives, and those with benefit of learning them without, who labour with their hands. Though 'tis nigh on fifty years since last I saw her, I hear her voice yet, so marked the impression she did make upon my youthful mind.

They were heady days for me, escaped from out my father's house, from tedious workshop labour, to see something of the world, and not yet bound in wedlock. And so they stay with me, glowing like distant jewels. And she most rare of all. For I did grow to love her like the mother that I was born without. And she, that did promise my father she would treat me like a daughter, did so, loving me likewise. And did instruct me as she would a daughter, had she but given birth to one.

Her words are with me yet, though she herself, poor lady, has long since turned to dust. She'd say, that in the kingdom of the blind the one-eyed man is king. And so we stumble blindly on, from mire to mire. Those who see further, looking with both their eyes, and not the I of self that looks asquint, of interest only, they are rare indeed, truly the visionaries of our time, unschooled though they may be, and lacking Latin.

She loved to talk so, and would have me listen. Such a spirit as I found in her was strange to me at first, I scarce durst credit it. Women have tongues, and thoughts, but lack the liberty to speak their minds, or lack the education to speak wisely. What had I heard till then? A scolding housewife merely, and an angry sister, both captives to their state. Likewise our old servant, full of ancient super-

45

stitions and old saws. Each spoke some partial truth perhaps, but spoke it partially, blinkered by custom. But my lady loved to talk for talking's sake. Such great eyes she had, would sparkle with the joy of argument when the mood was on her. For she found pleasure in the following of her thoughts.

Aye, pleasure, daughter. Have you not seen a skylark dip and swerve, for joy of being alive? Thus was she, on happy days, and thus her thoughts, when she was in the mood to follow them. That there were darks days also, I grant you, for she would swing from high to low. From thinking that which I had thought unthinkable, being answerable to no one but herself, to God and her own conscience, which gave her leave to speak; to black night fears, dark doubts, and melancholy. Then she would pace the floor, and have me walk with her, and speak of death and that which lay beyond, and tremble in her shift, and fall upon her knees, praying to her Saviour. For, so she said, this mood being upon her, we are in the dark, and that which we think conscience may delude us. What Hell must then await us, being wrong, our conscience but a snare to trap us into error, and we forever judged amongst the damned.

To hear her speak thus put the fear of God in me. Indeed, I know not which did fright me more, to hear her speak of Hell and Judgement Day, of being not elect and therefore cursed, or in her sprightlier mood, her daylight self, when she did scoff at long accepted wisdom and called it foolishness, or worse, hypocrisy. For might is right, she said, this you must know, whether in battle or within the house, beside your hearth. So Plato spake, that justice is no more than the interest of the stronger, and Lucan also. I think she said 'twas Lucan. I was

46

much in awe, having been taught that women were unfit for higher learning, being born to serve, not study. Which, when I spoke of it, did make her laugh most heartily. Books are their arsenal, she said, did I not tell you might is right? So they must keep us out of school, else fear for their dominion.

I hear her still. A tinker may see clearer than a king, yet end in jail for saying what he sees. Thus runs the world, she said, and I fear 'twill ever do so, whether the king be born to his estate or put there by the sword. 'Tis all one. For might is right, and those who have it think themselves elect of God, whether they rule in Westminster or a small house at Bunhill, put there by a pair of breeches and little else besides, like a cock in the farmyard crowing lustily by virtue of his comb. So we must flatter, bow and scrape, or take the consequence. Have you not seen how women speak to men, feeding their self-regard? Yes John, no John, if you say so husband. Though men do hate our tongues they hate them only when we speak truth, which they call scolding, being but the repetition of that which they would not hear. When we do oil and flatter they will hear us readily enough, and think us virtuous.

When she spoke thus, it did put me in mind of Mistress Betty, our stepmother. What did she ever do but carry idle tittletattle to his willing ears, and twist and turn the veriest trifle into some monster of iniquity, for her own ends? Which she has got, I think, being well set up in comfort. A man is ever a willing dupe when self-love sits at his elbow.

I spoke of this to my lady, having some bitterness yet in my heart. For I was young, and smarted still from hurts but lately got. It was she who instilled some pardon in my heart. It grieved her, she

47

declared, to see a man so great in stature conduct himself so pettily. As for your unkind stepmother, she said, her state is much like yours, though you think not. What other choice hath she, being born a woman, with neither face nor fortune to her name, but to keep house, and serve, and bide her time, her husband being old? Three previous daughters cannot serve her interest, but to consume her portion, being yet unwed and still within the house. She served her interest, who did but serve her husband, and saw in it but wifely duty, to keep his peace. He who accepts such service, so she said, 'tis he who is at fault.

Shall we not light a candle, being now so wealthy? It grows dark, and Urban not yet home. I think he has gone to the widow, for she keeps a good table, so I hear. A tasty stew would tempt him to sup with her, though her complexion is sallow. And by candlelight it may look well enough. I will stoke the coals, at least, to give us light and heat. Our old servant would say, whilst mending by the fire, if she had but had a farthing for every candle he did burn at nights, she could have lived and died a rich woman. Instead of stitching by a dying hearth, from which is to be got but poor eyes, sore thumbs, and poverty.

He let go the sole right of printing, else you and I might have done without charity to warm us this night. They say there are more copies sold now than ever he burnt candles, but the bookseller will give us nothing for being descended from him. So he grows rich, and we must labour to patch an old shirt. Yet I spoilt my eyes with reading to him, and oft took down the lines now printed in such numbers.

Virtue should be its own reward, I know, and

duty also, yet 'tis a hard principle, with but little justice in it. Even an ass will labour better with carrot than with stick, and we have souls that should be nurtured, that we may grow. My cousins, though they died poor, did yet have opportunity to profit from his learning. But there is little profit to be got from women's work, unless it is six feet of earth.

There, the shirt is done, but will not withstand much washing, so I think, for all my endeavour. 'Tis no wonder that she is miserly, my father's widow. It makes us niggards in our own behalf, if we can but earn by saving another's pence. Look at this poor patched shirt, for all my labour. A prudent wife, we say, meaning one who has a care to keep her husband's pence. Who will make do and mend, and scrimp and save, and call it wealth to have a silken gown and a few baubles to adorn herself. When Adam delved and Eve span, who was then the gentleman? But now our gentlemen have given over digging, being sent to college, and Eve yet sits and spins. This was another jest my lady told, who held that girls should have the like education as their brothers. Which some men of the time did hold, though not my father.

How easily he parted with his coin, that gentleman just now. And yet not born high, I think, but from the middling sort. He carries his wealth in his head, and gets a living by it. See you in him that thrift which should keep us from want? Why, he spends more on garnet buttons for his coat than we get in a year to keep us clothed and fed. He saves no candle ends nor mends a shirt thrice over.

But yet she knew how to manage matters, that shrew, to suit her purpose. For she would coddle his fancy with nice dishes and sweet puddings. Old men and babes are alike in this, that nothing will keep them so content as a tasty morsel. Dear Betty, he would say, as the steaming dish was put upon the table, so he could smell its odour close to him, his blind head alert to such sensation, everything I have goes to you when I die. Sniffing at cinnamon and spice, or a rich gravy, and smiling. It was a jest that ever went between them, she gratifying his appetite with her skill, and though he spoke in jest, in truth he spoke in earnest, reminding us and her, and all who heard him, that nothing was writ down concerning his last will and testament, and so could yet be altered. To hark thus ever on his goods and chattels, by word of mouth, whilst making yet no written testament, what was it but an everlasting bribe, a cajoling from this day to the next, to keep her kind to him? And so, though speaking seemingly in jest, he would remind her who had yet control, for all his age and disability. He kept her at his beck and call like a kite in the wind, having but to tug the string to make her do his bidding.

Though I had no liking for her, being a scolding shrew from first to last, I see how she was caught. Such petty tricks and turns are played when a man marries but to keep his house, and she to keep herself. This is no bonding betwixt like and like, and liking is not in it, nor goodly fellowship. So she is apt to fawn and flatter.

I thank my stars I was not wedded to a husband who could quote me Latin. You and I, though poor, and oft in need, have yet more dignity within our household. We are not thought a lesser being for labouring with our hands, our husbands doing likewise. They need our toil to prosper. But I would not have you wear yourself to a shadow. We shall get by this winter, even though the work is hard to come by.

Your father ever held that laws were writ in Latin but to fox the poor man in the dock. And though the practice ended with our late rebellions, we are as far now from plain language as before, lawyers making it their business to confuse us. For all the blood that was shed. That Rome was banished quite, this did give him some comfort in his latter years, but little else.

Yet my uncle died a Papist, that was the kindest man I ever knew. He held the freedom that was sought by men such as my father was but the liberty to be a tyrant within doors. So my father would have but conscience as his guide in ruling us.

I know nothing of law, daughter. But, as my uncle told it, the law provides that widows must be cared for, and offspring likewise. This your father thought but intermeddling, he said. And so I thought it best (and here his eyes would twinkle in the telling) to humour him, when he did speak of leaving all to Betty, as he would do when I did call on him, betwixt the law courts and returning home to Ipswich, thinking you and your sisters would be better served by doing nothing. And so we got a little when he died, the case coming to court, and probate being refused to Mistress Betty, for all her scheming. We got the portion that was due to us. Being but lately married to your father, though far off in Dublin, it proved a timely marriage portion.

A kind of obstinacy, I think, held him to the last, and would give him no rest. That he, an author and a scrivener's son, besides being elder brother to a lawyer of the Inner Temple, should leave no written will and testament is otherwise so passing strange as to defy all logic. And yet, being sound of mind, such wilfulness is surely nigh to blindness of another sort.

He was kind to us, our uncle Christopher. I hope, for his sake and mine, you will be mindful of his daughters, should they have need of you. Mary and Catherine grow elderly, as I do. Whilst they have each other for company they are content enough in Highgate. But I hope, one dying, you will not leave her sister comfortless and lonely. And they have been kind to you also, when you were a child. Being unmarried and childless, they made much of you, would kiss and fondle you, and give you sweetmeats. Too much, upon occasion, for your stomach.

Though I like not to depend upon charity, it is good to see so much coin together. I would a woman were paid in wages, and not in kind. It gives a kind of lift to the spirit, to hold such coins in the palm of your hand and think how you would spend them. Why, even a servant must be paid in wages. I think our little Liza should get new shoes with this, what think you? She grows apace, and those she has begin to pinch. What would you have, daughter, with these guineas? For they are yours to spend, I will not touch a penny. My needs are few, being old, and such garments as I have will see me out.

If Mr Addison had lived, he would have got me a pension, and I provided for. But the poor gentleman is dead, and there is no help for it. It is not much, is it, daughter, that we must needs cry charity at the end of a hard life with much labour in it? I thank God that you and Urban have been spared me, to be a comfort to me now. For though they call it labour to bring babes into the world, none pays us for it. Yet the world would go ill without us.

But that has ever been the way. You have heard your father speak of it, that nothing changes though it seems to do so. For he lived through those troublous times, and saw his kind deluded. We fought and died, he used to say, beguiled by promises of liberty. But those who led us, and would have us take up arms against the king, were more intent upon their property, on keeping what they had and getting more, and being spared such taxes as they would not pay. For property, they said, did give them rights within the kingdom, and we without had none. Such thanks we get for fighting of their battles, to be sent home unpaid and unrewarded.

I am no politician, daughter, and have but little knowledge of affairs. Yet I cannot think it right the country should belong only to those who have an interest in it, as they say, meaning they presently own much of it, and would have it remain so. So feudal lords would keep us yet in Norman bondage, which none think right. And yet their freeholds give them a voice we lack. So masters would rule their servants, men their wives, and this they call a just state, and democracy? All men are one in this, though in nought else.

Yet have we tongues, and will wag them, give us but half a chance. I have oft heard it spoken of, with pride by women, and with scorn by men, that when the troubles started wives and gentlewomen, and others of the female sex, took it upon themselves to petition the House of Commons, as did likewise such common riffraff as boatmen, porters and apprentices. There was much complaint made of this rabble by those who held discourse within. Go to your kitchens, so the crowd was told, it is not fitting for women to show themselves thus publicly, you have no business here. Yet they made answer, that Christ died to save both sexes, that women are sharers in the common calamities of both Church and state, suffer as much, and were held in Newgate also, for refusing to go against conscience, and so brought about the bishops' downfall.

As for the meaner sort, were they not soldiers in the war, fighting many a grievous battle for their betters, at risk of life and limb, and should they do this without some recompense? That promises were made I doubt not, and if not made, inferred. For who will fight but to maintain another's interest, and then go home unpaid? Our middling sort did not think enough on this, when they summoned up the poor. For men that have no land, nor freehold to their name, may yet find they have a conscience all their own. And being likewise taxed, in shillings, giving quarter, and in blood, will find they are unwilling to be ruled, since they have had no vote.

No, the middling sort did not think on that, when they summoned up their tenants to form troops of horse, and merchants got their servants and apprentices to put up barricades in city streets, aye, and their wives and children too. For when the war was won and the king's army routed, there were the poor, those selfsame soldiers, clamouring about the streets, unwilling to go home unpaid. They were the debtors now, the prosperous gentry grown fat on Church lands, the merchants newly rich, and now victorious. An army must be paid, kings have ever known that, for which they have sought taxes, whether ship money or any other levy. Now the rebels found it out. Soldiers must be paid, if not in coin, then in some other kind. Such promises as will send men into battle with psalms upon their lips are great promises indeed, and must be kept.

Freedom was the watchword, yet would their commanders send them home with empty bellies. Freedom to go without is scarce worth fighting for, but now it seemed that those with property would keep it for themselves, and give no wider share in saying how the kingdom should be governed, for fear of losing it.

Soldiers, being unpaid, did roam the streets, and turned their pistols on their officers, crying 'money, money, money'. Our old servant would speak of those times. Nothing but rumours running through the streets, apprentices rioting either for king or Parliament, and bands of reformadoes, as they were known, disbanded soldiers, roving about the city, intent on mischief. It was a time, she said, when a woman was fearful of her life in the getting of a dozen eggs or a pound of candles, and few sellers coming to the door.

I never heard so much talk as then went on, she'd tell me, as I sat shelling peas or some such task. I liked to help her in the kitchen, more than to do my father's bidding, for she would gossip of old times in such a manner as made them live for me. So much of arguing as went on then, she'd say, on the rights and wrongs of it. Every man was become a lawyer, though he could scarce write his own name, and each woman who could read the Bible for herself a preacher or a prophetess of things unfolding. And some did fear the army, saying this was no rule of law to flout the Commons thus, and others holding that the army did represent the people more than Westminster, it being elected but by very few, the men of property. As for me, she'd say, 'twas all one, being but a woman and a servant, and thus excluded by both factions from having any say. But the price of milk was high, and butter barely to be found.

And then the army marched into the city with sprigs of laurel in their hats, their leaders with them, each riding at the head of his regiment. Though gossip had it that they went but with the tide, having no other choice. The storm being unleashed, they now must ride it, like a straw atop a wave. Cromwell and Fairfax might look proud upon their mounts, yet were they led from behind. For he who would dance must pay the fiddler, or dance a gallow's jig.

Such a pother, she would say, and with nothing to show for it at last. For when all was said and done, one faction was as like to t'other as a pea to its neighbour in the pod. The army, having won the day and taken London, against the wishes of their paymasters, that had no pay to give them, took to debating the future of the kingdom on t'other side the river, as though elected so to do, if not by Magna Carta then by swords and muskets. All shall have a voice they said, in choosing parliament, all but women, servants and beggars. On hearing which I said, bring back our king, but alas, soon his head was off, this course being voted for by force of arms, for all who would say nay were purged from out the House, and kept from entering.

I was but a child during those times, and saw and heard with but little understanding. Yet I recall that all who spoke of it, as afterwards your father, spoke of it as a time of hopes dashed or deferred, of grievous disappointment. From this I do deduce that we must have a care of meddling too much in things politic, for fear of losing that which we would gain, and more besides upon occasion. You speak rashly, as those yet young will do, lacking experience, but desiring justice. Yet it is hard to come by in this world, and blood spilt will scarce get it for us.

And if humility is a Christian virtue, 'tis ever lacking in affairs of state. For men that thought themselves elect of God, and come to perfect grace, were but imperfect, and prone to error. Thus conscience can beguile us, so my uncle said. Take but authority away and all is turmoil: the law must be obeyed or we are lost. My father, on the contrary, despised the rabble, and thought it right that those few men who heard the voice of God should rule by force if need be. Yet who can say that what he hears is God, and not his own voice whispering that which he would hear? And so there will be a mighty babble at the last, and much confusion.

I think my lady Merian spoke but the truth when she did say self-interest ever rules. So landlords feared to lose what they had got, and tradesmen thought themselves but poorly used, for who it is, they said, makes for our country's wealth? Meaning not such as you or I, that do but bring babes into the world, and wash and mend and mind the pot, but those whose industry is paid in coin. So, I think, each faction feared to lose, or not to gain that which they hoped for by their strife. But those with nothing, landless beggars, who did but seek a patch of common ground to grow their crops, so as to fill their empty stomachs, these were turned away and soon sent packing, first by soldiers, then by all who lived nearby.

But our interest, so she opined, is in our fellow men, and women too, that all should have enough. I can but eat so much, sleep in one bed, wear one gown at a time, yet others starve, sleep on the bare ground, and shiver out of doors whilst I enjoy this surfeit. And yet, she'd say, those who have enough, or more than a sufficiency, are wont to speak as though it were a virtue, not their good fortune. As though it were industry alone, and righteousness, that spared them beggary, not privilege of birth, inheritance, or sex or mere rude health. It is not by dint of virtue we are wealthy, nor poor through lack of it. This is but an argument against charity, so those without may beg unheard.

For though the good Book tells us that the slothful will not plough in winter and must beg in summer, it tells us also that he that hath mercy upon the poor lendeth unto the Lord, and the Lord will recompense him that which he hath given. For charity is but a kind of interest, and brings us profit of a greater kind. And though it seems not so, it is self-interest to think not just on self: not to gain reward in Heaven, but here upon this earth. For we must dwell upon this earth together, and whilst my brother and my sister want for food and shelter, we shall not undo the sin of Adam, nor shall there be a Paradise regained upon this earth, nor Second Coming.

It was for this the war was fought, or so the Generalissimo would have them think, that risked their lives for him. And so my father thought, aye, and yours likewise, that what began upon the battlefields of England, God giving victory, should quickly bring about the final transformation through the world. And yet, no sooner was the victory given, and unpaid soldiers seeking their reward, then their officers would have them go home hungry, in body and in soul.

England belongs, declared their chief of men, the General, to men of property. Those who have no interest in it other than to have been born in it, and by virtue of breathing, can have no say in how it shall be governed, for such a course would lead to anarchy, each man desiring what he had not got, and striving for it through the ballot. He that had heard the voice of God in going into battle, in bringing such upheavals to our land, would now cry order order, and go home go home, enough it is enough.

We speak of God, and goodness, so my lady said, but in our hearts is naught but property. And though we pray for the coming of His kingdom, we rather fear to lose that which we have, than get a better world here down below. For those with much know it unjustly got, whilst others go without. Else would we face the judgement of the Lord, his Second Coming, with equanimity. However it may come, whether by stealth and slow democracy, or some miraculous event.

You must have patience here on earth, I fear. 'Tis no use fretting. I hear your father's voice still. We seek but an honest competence, he'd say, yet laws, wars and taxes, unprotected trade and cheap importing do take it from us. How can we prosper if we have no say in how the country is governed?

I fear his life was but a tedious, unavailing search for betterment. First, being a Fifth Monarchist, he sought it here in London, and sought in vain, the Good Old Cause betrayed. Then in Dublin, where trouble but followed us in King James's time, and back to London when King James was ousted. Some would have the cause now won, King Billy coming, but 'tis as unlike the vision your father nursed in youth as our back yard is to Adam's garden.

And so it will remain, I fear. We must take charity where we find it, and not grumble needlessly, that some have garnet buttons and we patch fustian. I was born into a time when great beliefs did flourish, and men saw glorious visions. Such hopes were dashed, and now we think it foolish, a dream of Paradise not to be found this side the grave. You, who come after, know the hope is lost. Though whether 'tis better to be born with hope and lose it, or to come into this world a cynic, and so get what you can, I know not.

Whatever is, is right, is now the current thought. They do betray my father that think so, for all their worship of him. And those who must beg out of doors this cold night know otherwise, though they have no shillings to spend at the bookseller.

And Urban not yet back. I think he must have gone to sup with the widow. Shall we stoke the fire, daughter, or let it die? And what's for supper? Daughter? Are you awake? Poor child, she's fast asleep, and no wonder. She should never have got up so soon after her delivery. But yet she would not hear me, when I told her to stay abed.

FOUR

Y OUR NAME, SIR? I have no recollection of it, and
the professor has not been here for some time.
I fear you come at an inopportune moment, my
daughter being unwell. She took sick this morning
and I have scarce left her side. I would not be
inhospitable, but we live in poor circumstances,
with an only servant, who is young and clumsy.
There is much disorder in the house, and this room
not fit for callers.

Will you not return at some more fitting time?
You see we are all at sixes and sevens, with the
floor not swept. My daughter's pregnancy does not
go well with her, and I am anxious. She has lost
two babes already, and is very low.

Then pray, take a seat. I hope it is not dusty. The
child is slow at her tasks, but today must be excused.
Two hands can only do so much, and she has had
more than her share this day. I would offer you a
dish of tea but there is no one to prepare it, and
now I think on it, no tea neither. I find it very dear
still, and so we buy it sparingly. My daughter had
the last of it an hour ago.

She is in the fourth month, but the sickness will
not leave her. I think she is fearful to lose this child
also, which makes her fretful. I was in the same case
myself as a young woman, losing many children in

61

infancy, so I understand her thoughts. Such fears serving no purpose, we must strive to master them, but 'tis easier said than done. But she has one child living, the prettiest girl you ever did see. She is with a neighbour at present, her mother being sick, else you could see her.

Relics, sir? I can think of none, unless you would call me such, being old, and the only one of his children now living. My poor sisters are both dead this long while, and neither had offspring to survive them. Mary died unwed and Anne in childbed, her infant also.

You see how poorly we live here. Some bits and pieces of household furniture were sent to me in Dublin after his death, but not brought back on our return, since they did not warrant the expense of shipping. My father's silver seal I gave to my daughter on her wedding day. It is hers to dispose of, not mine. I will not trouble her in her condition, else you could ask her yourself, though I know what the answer would be. It has an eagle on it, with two heads and wings spread wide, his family arms.

For other relics, as you call them, you must visit my stepmother. She is yet living, in Nantwich, and I doubt not but has a great horde of such mementoes.

Books, sir? Look around you. You see how sparsely this room is furnished. Does it look like a gentleman's parlour? We have but the bare necessities here, and no room for such luxury, had they been left me. My father gave much space to his books, but here we are packed tight as oysters in a barrel, the house being small, and my son also lodging with us.

No study in this house, nor rows of books. You

have come on a fool's errand if you thought otherwise. Many were sold before his death, my father having no heirs that he would recognise to make good use of them. We were but girls, and thus unfit. And yet I spoilt my eyes in reading to him, and have worn spectacles since I left his house. A paltry inheritance.

But the bookseller has grown rich, I hear, with bringing out his work in new editions, having got the sole right of printing for nought. I would I had a little of those earnings now, to get comforts for my ailing daughter. You see how little he thought on us, to let it go so lightly. Was it not a life's work like any other, and would a man give away house and land, a lifetime's capital, ignoring his children's needs? Had his father done likewise, he might have been apprenticed to labour with his hands, as I was, and died a pauper, as like as not. And so goodbye to study.

Forgive me, sir. You did not come to hear me speak of such matters. I fear I cannot help you, and you must leave with nothing. You come at a bad time, and I am anxious. I have heard there is much profit to be got from autographs, and similar mementoes of famous men. You may have something in my hand if you wish, for, being blind, I wrote at his dictation, but I think this is not to your purpose. A pity, else I might buy new shoes for my daughter's child, and more tea to ease her discomfort.

No, sir, I have told you once already, the seal was given to my daughter as a gift, and I know she would be unwilling to part from it. You would but see it? I left her sleeping, and will not disturb her on such an errand. Now, if you will excuse me, there is much to do within the house. Our sole servant is gone to market, and I must to the kitchen.

But now I think on it, I do have some mementoes of a kind. My cousin Edward, when he died, left me a box of papers belonging to my father. They are of little interest now, else they had long been given away or sold for profit. For despite the learning he received from my father my cousin did not prosper and was oft impoverished. Authorship without good fortune is not a life to choose, I think, and in this my father may have done my cousins some disservice, for all his schoolmastering. Great gifts bring great rewards, mostly in Heaven, but small talents little coin. As for Grub Street, 'tis only fit for worms and insects, so my father said, yet did both his pupils sink to it. My uncle Christopher ever felt they had been better employed learning some honest trade, or going to the university, or to the inns of court to study law, as he did. Such education as your father gave them, he would say, made them unfit for all but that for which they had no gift, and no true calling. He said it kindly, being a kindly man, but meant it in good earnest.

The papers? I cannot at this moment recollect where they are put. My daughter moved the box some time ago, I do recall. We were spring-cleaning at the time. But where she put it I do not recollect. And it is scarce worth hunting for, being of no interest. There is nought in the box but pamphlets, old political stuff no mortal gives a fig for now.

This is your particular passion? Is that so? Then you are rare indeed, for few now value my father for his politics, or study his times. My late husband also was much engaged with such interests, being my senior by many years, and having the hot blood of youth in him during those years of turmoil. But both spoke bitterly at the end, feeling themselves betrayed. He was a weaver, not a poet, you understand, and so his hopes were more particular.

I have heard him many a time in his last illness, musing on early dreams and late despair. For he died poor as he began, for all his industry. We cried for freedom, liberty, he'd say, yet what was it, when all is said and done? But the freedom to bob about like flotsam on the waves, or leaves blown in the wind. Without just government 'tis but the freedom of the wilderness where savages do roam, to kill and pillage as they please. Not a fruitful garden, as God intended, where all is order, all sufficiency. For those who have get more, this being the law of interest, whilst those without stay poor, for all their labour.

The box, sir? I will search for it presently. The rooms are so higgledy-piggledy just now, my daughter being unwell and the servant disorderly on account of her youth, I scarce know where to look. I would tell you what I know of my father's opinions but, being a mere child during those troubled times, I recollect little, and saw all things with a child's eye. So I oft confused his bitterness concerning all that had gone amiss in the great world with his domestic discontents, being more familiar. Was it my mother who had brought about the Fall and troubled times? Was my childish failure to obey his every wish the reason for the turmoil in the streets, and his displeasure? It almost seemed so, for in childhood guilty thoughts do grow like giants, to seize on every trifle.

And yet I heard much talk in the house from my earliest years, of what had been before my birth. That which I recollect may be of use to you. We had a servant, sir, who had been with my father many years and knew him as a boy, having first served his parents. Which fact, she thought, did give her licence to speak her mind on each and every matter, which much displeased my father, who was wont to wax sarcastical on women's tongues. But to me and my sisters, lacking a mother to beguile our ears, her gossip was ever welcome. She told us how, when the war first started, the whole city was rife with talk on future government. I think that she herself must have been infect with those unruly times, for ever after she did blab her thoughts to those that did employ her, whether they would hear them or no.

There were those, she said, who though mere servants, would not wash dishes for conscience's sake upon the Sabbath. This was not my way, she said, since our stomachs rumble as loudly on that day as any other, and infants cry, and ashes smut the hearth. But I will speak my mind when conscience tells me, and none shall shut me up. This was her way, sir, and I did love her for it, though at the last . . .

I will get the pamphlets directly. I think the box is in the back room, by the coals. My daughter had a mind to use them for tinder, but I would not have it. Indeed, it is a wonder so many yet remain, since our old servant roused my father's ire by burning some of them during that first winter of the civil war, there being no coals come in from Newcastle, for the roads were cut off by troops. Having nought else to cook the dinner with, she burned them, and would not be rebuked. To her mind 'twas all hot air, and fit as such only for cooking stews. Besides, she said, what else was there to do? You cannot cook without fire, and fire with neither wood nor coals within the house is hard to come by. Did they not teach you that at your university? You go upstairs and put the world to rights within your study, and leave me to my business in this kitchen. 'Tis hungry work you do, and I doubt you have the stomach for eating raw, like savages. What my father said to this I know not. 'Tis possible the tale got more pert with the telling, as we do oft embroider our little triumphs against authority.

Now, for the box. I hope there are yet some pamphlets remaining. Our servant needs watching, and is apt to follow her own whims. I have seen her use my Bible as a stepping-stone when cleaning shelves. Do not touch it, sir. The lid is smutty and must be wiped. I would not have you dirty your hands.

I must put on spectacles for this. *Tyrannical Government Anatomized* – will you look through it? They are all much in this vein, as I recall. Those who come to visit me of late find such matter tedious and of little moment, so the box has gathered dust. They seek the poet, thinking him sublime, and ignore the rest. But, since you say you have an interest in things political, you will wish to study what yet remains within.

A Discourse Shewing in What State the Three Kingdoms Are in. Printed in sixteen forty-one, almost a hundred years since. How curious it is to look on it. Printed at the sign of the Cock. This was the fashion then in publishing, and few put their names to that which they had written, fearing reprisal. But this you know, how foolish of me to lecture you thus.

A Slingshot Against all Tyrants. And here a few receipts. Two yards of fustian, a pound of candles. A remedy for fever – this is in my sister's hand. She's long since dead. I had not thought to find such things here. Like dry leaves from a vanished season. The ink has changed colour with the years.

What's that you say? That censorship broke down, the war beginning? 'Tis little wonder then, that such a spate of pamphlets issued forth.

My father did welcome such liberty of speaking. But he was not so within doors. My poor sister did suffer much from this, turning rebellious at his dominion. Each protest did but harm her cause, and to endure in silence was not in her nature. I was once companion to a lady who held that men do differ in their public and their private life, cry freedom for themselves, but not their wives and children.

The Nation's Tongue Unleash'd. And it was, from all I have heard. Servants and beggars were as like to clack as any preacher. Printed in Goldsmith's Alley. So much commotion to so little end, think you not? Each title lengthier than the last, like a kite's tail in the wind. Indeed, I have heard our old servant confess that some were used as such by my cousins, and a sore whipping they got for it, which terrified our mother and had sent her running, if nothing else had driven her hence.

She meant my mother, sir, who died at my birth. You have doubtless heard the scandalous gossip of her going home and failing to return when sent for. And then my father's pamphlets on divorce, which brought the greater scandal to our name. I know not if they are here. But they have been thought so notorious that you must be familiar with them. They had unlooked for consequences which my father much misliked, thinking the freedom which he sought himself to be another's licence. It seems a preacher dwelling in Bell Alley abjured her husband, called him unsanctified, and took to living with another man, a preacher also, who had a wife yet living, and many children. So they practised what my father preached, having studied his doctrines.

It seems that others also took my father's word as law and laid aside their spouses to take another, thinking that conscience only was their guide, which was in fact mere lust or lack of liking. This much displeased my father, so my uncle had it. He was a lawyer and outlived my father by many years. For that which he called freedom for himself was not intended for the lower sort, for an unregenerate rabble, nor for women.

My uncle never spoke of it within his hearing, but only after his death. Freedom without responsibility, he'd say, how can this be? If God gave us authority over wives, as doth the law, they are also given in our charge for better or for worse, as children are, and servants. Shall I then put my wife aside because her face mislikes me, or she lacks conversation? Did I marry her for this or, if I did, had I not time enough to chat with her, and try her at my leisure?

Thus spoke my uncle, ever the lawyer. I can hear him still. The law is yet the law, and must be obeyed. He thought it wrong for any man to put himself above it for conscience merely. Else each becomes a law unto himself and chaos follows. These are nice points of philosophy, not easily resolved. I would hear your opinion. What if the law be wrong, must we obey it? Yet, if each man takes his conscience as his guide he is like to become a law unto himself, and conscience often tells us that which we would hear. I know not how to resolve this riddle.

What think you, sir, that have an interest in things political? What is the orthodoxy now? I believe that we must suffer in this world, whether it be the vagaries of fortune, bad harvests, falls in trade, or those failings in a spouse we cannot mend. But I am a mere woman, and have not studied. That the Fall must be redressed, this was widely held during my father's time, and many thought that suffering meekly, and mere virtue, would not do it. The Norman yoke, which took away our freedoms, did so by violence, and so must be violently opposed, if need be. And yet, if each man has his voice, aye, and woman too, to speak his mind and follow it with action, how can ought but disorder follow?

Those who rule, I think, must seek consent, else turmoil will result. Is this not your opinion? Whether it be within the household or the state, 'tis all one. A wife must be wooed with kindness, and he who would have children must be a father. This my uncle understood more nearly than my father, for my cousins loved him dearly, and my aunt also. I never saw strife betwixt them, or serious argument.

He called us unkind daughters at the last, yet got but what he gave, unkindness for unkindness, harsh words for harsh. We give our freedom gladly to those we love, and serve them willingly. This I know, having been both wife and mother. For freedom is but a notion, when all is said and done.

Do not touch the box, sir, you will soil your fingers. If you are in haste it will keep for another occasion. As I told you, there is nothing of value in it, unless it be for curiosity. I would you had come at a more opportune time, and given us warning of your visit. I might then have found the papers of most interest. No, you may not remove them to your lodgings.

Now you have led my thoughts astray. What was I searching for when you distracted me? I know I had it in mind to show you a particular document. Ah yes, here I have it, the ordinance of sixteen forty-three against seditious books and pamphlets, issued by Parliament. It orders that no book, pamphlet or paper shall be printed, bound or put to sale unless first licensed according to the ancient custom. Will you peruse it? As I recall, it speaks of searches to be made for unlicensed printing presses, and for authors and printers of such unlicensed works to be apprehended and brought before the House of Commons.

Rebels turned rulers do mislike freedom of speech as much as those they ousted, for free opinions may be well enough but become a great inconvenience once in government. So my father found to his cost, in turning censor, despite his noble words defending liberty of speaking. For fools will crow as loudly as a prophet, and make a pandemonium in place of order.

I am but a woman, and our tongues must be still whoever rules. What are your views in the matter? I would gladly hear them. My late husband judged the middling sort no better than the rest, in terms of knowing truth. If truth is not in privilege and rank, forever fixed, why should it stop with men of property and leave out all the rest?

He was a weaver and, during those troubled times, a mere apprentice with but little education. And yet, he said, I could read the good Book as well as any man, and understand its meaning right enough. So why should such as I be silenced? Was the war fought for this? But our old servant took an earthy view, and saw in this but chaos, if all would rule and no one obey. A fine thing for the chicken, she'd say, if it could cite Scripture to prove that it should not have its head wrung off for the pot, but a poor prospect for those who would eat their supper. And tell me not to be a silly child, to feel pity for the poor dead bird in her lap, its feathers being plucked.

I think my father was no hypocrite, for all he found himself a licenser at last, that had preached freedom of the presses, and of opinion. You must not think so. He feared to lose that which had been gained at such great cost. Yet progress by oppression is but a poor way forward, and 'tis little wonder many thought themselves betrayed.

Men, when they cry liberty, and would have the freedom of opinion to defend it, mean only to their own kind, and never to their foes. Else had my father given the like freedom to Papists, whom he loathed above all others. Yet he did not so. 'Tis human nature. Men who cry liberty of speech silence their wives and daughters without a thought, and those who serve them.

What's that you say? We cannot give liberty of printing to those who would deprive us of our liberties? I see you have indeed studied my father, for I know this to have been his opinion. Forgive me, sir, for to be frank I had taken you to be something of an impostor, and here for gain. I have made you blush, and I am sorry for it. 'Tis I who should do so, but my cheeks are too old to change colour.

'Tis an argument I would fault. Can mere opinion enslave us, if we be free? Surely our liberties, if they be firm, can withstand some knocks, and suffer little hurt. To stop our ears for fear of hearing seems foolish, since we must know the argument in order to refute it.

Was it not Ulysses who stopped his ears so he should not hear the sirens' song? I think so, though all my learning is but secondhand, and rusty now with lack of use. We live in modern times, now reason rules, not superstitious fear of magic, as it did in times of old. I think we need not fear to be beguiled, and stop our ears with wax, and tie us to the mast to sail a steady course. If we are bound for truth we shall not waver, and God will see us safely into port.

But let us to the box, it is not yet empty. Here it says that every man and woman are by nature equal, and have been so since the time of Adam and Eve. This is a red rag indeed, to set the bull by the horns. None of them having by nature any authority one over another, but merely by mutual agreement or consent. All lawful powers reside in the people, for whose good all government was ordained. Know you this pamphlet? The first page has gone astray. Lilburne, you say? Was he not put in prison by Parliament? 'Tis little wonder. They did not fight the war for this.

I know such sentiments were little to my father's liking. He thought the great mass unregenerate, blind to the merits of godly men, and too easily swayed by evil orators. It is not agreeable, he said, that such persons should ever be free. However much they may brawl about liberty, they are slaves, and deserve not a government of their own choosing, since they will never choose wisely.

Yet God gave us presses so the poor should learn to read, not just the middling sort, and there is no way back from that. Else had He kept His truth locked up in monasteries, and kept us popish to the last. So my husband thought, and many like him. And if we read, we think, and know our minds, there is no way back from that neither, for all their ordinances. Why, once it was forbidden to read the good Book, the very lifeblood of our truth, and source of all we know. And for why? So those who ruled by force of arms should keep us cowed, and ever in subjection.

Freedom can be abused, I doubt not, and partial knowledge is a dangerous thing. Yet who can say he has a hold on truth, and knows in all things better than his neighbour? What is sauce for the goose is sauce for the gander and, if conscience rules, mine is as good as any man's.

I had forgot how much was stored within this box. We live in other times, and such old debates have little meaning now. It makes me sad to think such turmoil of opinion was all in vain. I would not have you think me a friend to anarchy, and yet I see here something we have lost. You are young, belonging to a time more cynical, but I am a child of my time, and recall such hopes I once heard spoken of with some regret still at their passing.

You see how variable these pamphlets are, in voice and in opinion. Liberty should be a garden, so I think, where many flowers do flourish, all shapes, all scents, all hues, but orderly and trim, with no rank weed strangling its fellows. I do not like the age we live in now, finding it hard and unchristian. The wealthy are richer than ever they were in my youth, but with less regard for those who are poor. And love themselves for their good fortune, when they should love God.

Believe me, sir, I have seen much in a long life, and know whereof I speak. At the bottom of the box, as I remember, lie those papers I thought most remarkable. They have a kind of poetry to my ears, however much my father must have despised them. How like you this, if I can read it yet – 'the same spirit that hath lain hid under flesh, like a corn of wheat for an appointed time, under the clods of earth, is now sprung out and begins to grow a fruitful vine, which shall never decay'. And further on – 'This is the kingdom of God within man. This is the grain of mustard-seed, which is little in the beginning, but shall become a mighty tree.' I see you smile, and indeed, I never yet saw a mustard-seed become a tree. 'Tis humble stuff, I grant you, yet if words can move us, these will surely do so, despite reason. Besides, my father, for all his erudition, had greater errors in his work than this, but was readily pardoned for it by those who estimate his vision, despite cosmology.

And here's another by the same hand – 'all places stink with the abomination of self-seeking teachers and rulers. For do not I see that everyone preacheth for money, counsels for money and fights for money, to maintain particular interests? And none of these three, that pretend to give liberty to the creation, do give liberty to the creation; neither can they, for they are enemies to universal liberty; so that the earth stinks with their hypocrisy, covetousness, envy, sottish ignorance and pride.' This forthright tone is much to my liking. 'The common people are filled with good words from pulpits and council tables, but no good deeds; for they wait and wait for good and for deliverances, but none comes . . . Many that have been good housekeepers (as we say) cannot live, but are forced to turn soldiers and so to fight to uphold the curse, or else live in great straits of beggary.'

This was written in sixteen forty-nine, the king being lately dead, and I have little quarrel with it even now. It has the ring of truth to it, and to this day it touches me. A plain truth plainly spoken, and the better for all that. Poor people need no scholars to understand this. 'Tis as plain as a pike-staff, surely, and as purposeful. Yet who now reads Winstanley? I fear, sir, we care more for flourishes and rhyming than honest matter in these days.

We talk of troubled times, but forget the hope that was in them. No man can speak now in this fashion, with daily expectation of a new Paradise on earth, not just in England, but spreading thence across the world in a great reformation. I fear that younger authors now do turn to ancient stories not for truth, as was my father's way, but merely to divert a passing hour for those with too much leisure. So naiads frolic in the grove, and Troy must fall in rhyming couplets to amuse a lady. You see I am yet my father's daughter, and look for meaning.

I was taught that ancient stories, having their roots in truth, are not mere toys to play with, and dress in pretty words. Good and evil, light and dark, are locked in combat from time's beginning to our own, and Satan is as formidable now as ever in the past, and takes seductive forms. Yet who now thinks this way amongst our younger authors? Grown rich with privilege, untouched by war, they pander to a pampered readership, who think that Hector died to give them sport within their drawing rooms.

Reason is now the watchword, and unreason walks in fancy dress, tripping in metric lines. The world is a great clock that strikes the hours, and God has long since vanished, so it can take its course. Now virtue has no grace, and fancy rules where true imagination's long since lost.

I know how it goes amongst fine folks, in the smart quarter of town, although I live here in Spital-fields. You need not gainsay me, or look startled. But alas, the real world in which the poor must struggle rumbles ever on in the same old way, and this man speaks to me most potently with simple words, as a seer should. What is vision, if not the power to see for others, that are blinded by the world, and earthly things? So my father thought, in knowing he had lost his eyes to see more clearly. He doubted not his gift had come from God, to be used seriously, and not for sport.

Now the presses roll merrily enough, without let or hindrance. Yet to give such poets licence is but to despise them, words being mere playthings. They do no harm that seek to do no good, and but line their pockets to amuse.

I can read your thoughts, sir. You think I speak as the old do, ever judging past times better than the present. So Eve spoke, I doubt not, grown old with Adam in the wilderness. But the times grow worse, for all the new-fangled luxuries the wealthy now enjoy. So many carriages rumbling through our streets, yet beggars still a-plenty, the rich growing richer and the poor yet poorer. The advances of mankind are ever in creature comforts, but a new Heaven and a new earth are as far from us as ever they were. Who now thinks to see a Second Coming, to save us from our woes? Or labours for it? Whatever is, is right, is now the cry, and the Devil take the hindmost.

But we must be thankful for such freedoms as we enjoy. You are right to say so. Had it been my youth, I would not be gossiping freely with you, being required to keep silent. Women were much subdued. Is it not fearsome, the ordinance on printing you have in your hand? To have fought a war in the name of liberty of conscience, and then come down to this? That my father had little liking for the suppressing of other men's works I doubt not, you are right in this. Yet did he set his mind to it and lend his name, thinking the ends did justify the means. What think you of this doctrine? It was much in vogue then. I have heard him cite Ovid on the matter. But the end, sir, was not good.

I have heard my uncle say, he would rather be ruled by a hereditary lord than be subject to the rule of saints, the self-elect of God, as he would call them. That it was indeed a dangerous manner of ruling was proved by the outcome. Did not Cromwell kneel and pray before each battle, and see the hand of God in victory? So might was right, and so it followed, as the night the day, we should be ruled but by a single person. For the Lord Protector would shut each parliament almost as soon as he had declared it open, its members not doing that which he would have them do, or not doing it fast enough. For one man in his wisdom can decide in a trice what several hundred will argue on for weeks and months, and then, perhaps, fail to agree. I have been told he tried to rig the outcome of each election in advance, and yet would grow impatient if even these tame ciphers, puppets merely, did not do his bidding with sufficient speed.

How this should differ from what went before – I mean the king – I know not. My father, though uneasy, chose to speak of an unruly mob that must be governed, so the few were not deprived of their just liberty. But the common sort he so despised could see what they had got for their trouble, but a king with another name.

And then, sir, I ask myself – can we be saved despite our choosing? If God thought it fit to give our first parents in Eden free will to choose betwixt good and evil, though they chose the worst, is it meet for men, however good or great in wisdom, to give us less of liberty? I cannot think that this is the way to redemption.

Although I was scarce out of my cradle the first time that Cromwell put an end to Parliament, the manner of it was such, it could not but be part of common gossip ever after. He took with him a party of soldiers and appeared within the House dressed only in a plain black coat and worsted stockings, and though he began by speaking calmly enough he soon became enraged. They say he paced the floor as though he were a madman, kicking the ground and shouting, calling the members whoremasters and drunkards, one man corrupt, another scandalous to the profession of the Gospel. I say you are no Parliament, he shouted, ordering the soldiers to break up the sitting, and fetch the Speaker down from his chair.

Rule by a single person, it was called, who could not rule himself. Is it any wonder there was so much gossip? It seems there was a kind of devilish fury in him, which he said came from God. He called the mace a bauble, one man but a juggler, and told his officers he had not sought to have done this, but, perceiving the spirit of God so strong upon him, could do no other.

Some wag put a note on the door, saying this House was now to let, unfurnished. The city being full of rumours, Cromwell was suddenly sedulous to please all parties, even malignants. He took to visiting churches with a big prayer book under his arm, declaring that the Almighty had inspired him. And he would take umbrage if people did not doff their hats to him in public places, as they had formerly done in the presence of the king.

The Rump having been dispatched in such rude fashion, the Barebones followed, this being no parliament at all, but such men as Cromwell could call upon to vindicate his own authority, including members of his own family, and army officers under him. This was to be the coming together of saints, to bring about Christ's kingdom here on earth. God, he told the assembly thus brought together, doth manifest it to be a day of the power of Christ. They were a chosen body, so he said, at the edge of promises and prophecies. Which was, so gossip had it, but to make him king.

Yet even these saints, handpicked to do his bidding, did not prove sufficiently obedient, and after only a few months were sent packing by his musketeers. Living in state now, at Whitehall and Hampton Court, the Lord Protector would ever after call this assembly a sign of his weakness and folly, which had much teaching in it for the future. But it taught him, not to give a broader voice to the people, but rather to remove it utterly.

All this my father did concur in. You must know this, if you know aught. For, he said, if the greater part of the senate should choose to be slaves, or to expose the government to sale, ought not the lesser number to interpose, and endeavour to retain their liberty, if it be in their power? So he was also for the expelling of rotten members, as he called them, when the House was purged so the king could be voted to his death. But such topsyturvy logic has no merit. If I can see this, so can the common sort. A solo voice sings not in harmony by silencing the rest. And though my father ever thought it lawful that the few should rule the many, if the few had God and wisdom on their side, 'tis a foolish man who thinks himself forever in the right, and all the rest ungodly.

I would I had heard my late husband argue with

my father – there would have been a storm! But they did never meet, my father being deceased before our return to England. He heard only his own voice at last, so said Mr Clarke of the dictator, from listening only to those opinions concurring with his own. He was called His Highness now, that had begun life as plain Oliver, and ambassadors, on entering his chamber, would have to bow three times. But though he thought his own voice came from God, others found in it the voice of Satan, and called him Antichrist. A prophetess saw in him the Little Horn, a horrible excrescence in the head of the Beast, as described in Revelations, just as once his enemies had been revealed in like fashion. So a London apprentice saw in his titles the number of the Beast. And though such seers were thrown in prison, the discontent lived on.

A pretty pass things had come to, that the war should have been fought for this. Is it any wonder so many left these shores? My husband felt betrayed, and lost all hope. The wheel was come full circle when a merchant refused to pay custom duty, it not being authorised by Parliament, and was thrown in prison for it. You must know that the wars had begun in just this fashion, with Cromwell's kin refusing to pay ship money, taxes called for by the king without authority of Parliament. The merchant's lawyers pleaded his case so well that they must needs be thrown into the Tower for language destructive to the government. Whereupon the man pleaded his own case to such effect, the Chief Justice was utterly nonplussed. Delays and chicanery must be employed, else had the whole nation been free of taxes set by the Lord Protector.

I have heard my uncle speak of this case, he

being a lawyer. Many were uneasy, though serving Cromwell. For if an ordinance to levy taxes were not legal, then neither were any other ordinances brought in by the same means, including that for treason.

My uncle told me several judges were dispensed with, including the Chief Justice. He had little taste for what was then afoot, being of the royalist party. I know that judges can be partial in their judgements, like other men. My husband was ever of that opinion, thinking them prejudiced. And yet, sir, we must have some yardstick in our doings, must we not? If the king did wrong in governing without a parliament, I cannot but think the Lord Protector was likewise at fault.

How far can a yardstick bend without breaking? There was a saying in my youth – begin to build a wall crooked, and you must continue it awry till it falls. And use but crooked tools, to say 'tis straight. But two newspapers were permitted at this time, as you must know, both coming from the same pen, at the behest of Cromwell and his Council. They differed not a jot, though coming out on different days of the week. Their author being a turncoat, one who had formerly written for the king. Such crooked tools, sir – could he find no other? Few of his former friends would now defend him, there being but little left worthy to be defended.

A lie hath no legs, so said my uncle, but the Lord Protector would give himself a pair to stand with some authority. So he must needs call another parliament, more tame than those before. On this occasion, before issuing the writs, he locked up, not just royalists, but those of his opponents who had once been his friends. Even this was not enough. Having got them out of harm's way before the election, he had the door guarded by soldiers when the House did meet, admitting only those members with a ticket, so many found themselves excluded by his order, despite election.

To listen to the voices of the rabble was anarchy, my father held. To which my uncle would reply – what is civil war and regicide but anarchy? And I, being little more than a child caught between such contrary opinions, was much bewildered. But uncle, I queried, if the king be a tyrant, that takes away our Christian liberties, must he not be removed? And is every law good, that it must be obeyed? And if it be bad, should we not rebel, by force if need be? As for my father, I knew better than to bandy words with him. He would have taken it unkindly, both for my youth and sex, if I had dared to argue.

I have lived humbly, sir, and know humility, or so I think. We who are little people, leading small lives, do readily confess our faults and try to make amends. But the great men of this world, with great designs and mighty visions, thinking they cannot err, grow obstinate and will not change their course. But the best of men are but men at best, and 'tis our grace to know it.

I doubt not you are better versed in reading of the classics than I could ever be, having but used my eyes to read aloud in parrot fashion, and yet, as I recall, the ancients held it a grievous sin for men to think themselves like unto gods, or greater than they were, for which due punishment would follow. Is this not so? When a hero fell, the fault was in the hero, not in lesser mortals that did surround him and betray his cause. I fear my father, for all his years of study, learnt not this. Whether in things domestic or political, or in his version of the classic mode, he ever put the blame on lesser men and, if he could, on women, these being least of all. Delilah, Eve, or my poor mother, his daughters at the last.

Perfection is in God, not in ourselves, and for this reason Paradise was lost, and for no other. 'Tis but pride to think otherwise, and those most proud will fall the furthest, as the Bible teaches. Those who find perfection in themselves must surely end by condemning all others and, when things do go awry, blame all but themselves.

My religion has taught me this. As for my thoughts upon those times, they come from hearing others speak and thinking on them since. Being but a child my memories are oft childish. So I remember our old servant took a chopping knife to the head of a capon – this for King Noll then, she declared, adding, for he is as like to a king as this silly bird, and deserving to lose his head in the same fashion. Which must have been about the time that Cromwell was offered the kingship, though I had but a confused notion what a king might be, and little understanding of her scorn. So for a long time after I would think a king a crowing cock, his crown a coxcomb, having heard how he did lose his head and seen it for myself, our old servant hold his head aloft and, plucking off his feathers say, fine feathers make fine birds.

You laugh, sir, but a child will think thus, knowing no other way. You must know this for yourself. And what we hear in childhood stays with us forever, image and language both. What is coupled then will not be set asunder, reason how we will. So when I hear of crowns I think of coxcombs, and see the feathers fly within our kitchen, even whilst my reasoning mind knows otherwise.

There was much talk of Cromwell in his latter days, how he did not abjure fine feathers. This stays with me. Though dissuaded from taking of the kingship, he was invested with royal pomp as Lord Protector, robed in purple velvet, with sceptre, sword of state, and coronation chair. And like a cock he thought the sun did rise when he did crow, all other birds being silenced, and the last parliament of fowls dissolved.

So he was cock of the walk at last, crowing lustily, all others stilled, the press acts reinforced. But every cock must to the pot at last, for all his noises, and leave his yard behind. Who would protect them then, those foolish birds, who held that he alone would keep them from the fox and other harms? For he was old, and like to die, and what should follow after, many feared.

Men are but men at best, and cocks but cocks. They think too little on this, who would bear such burdens singly, and transform our world to make a better place. For we must hence, no one knows when, but that we go is sure. And if all our wisdom is pent within one body, what must follow when it dissolves? Without continuity all else is folly and idle turmoil.

I think 'twas for such reasons my uncle, and others like him, did favour the rule of law. Men die, as he would say, the law lives on, likewise the monarchy. A ruler crowned by force hath no just heirs, and force must follow him, if not before his death, then after. And for this reason there was talk of marrying Cromwell's daughter to King Charles's heir. A foolish notion, surely, for who would marry the offspring of their father's murderer? Aye, readily, was my sister's quick retort, but said in a low voice, so my uncle heard it not or, if he did, affected not to hear, being a kind of man who thought it best to be both deaf and blind upon occasion, in the cause of harmony.

Would that my father had been such, seeing his children with a father's eye, and not a judge's. For he would take each barb, each quick retort, at its face value, making no due allowance for those hurts got from his own tongue, which brought them on. A poor freedom, and a rougher justice, that lets a father say what he will, commanding silence and obedience in return. A judge would not pass sentence upon the veriest murderer, his case being unheard. Yet we were not heard, being unjustly accused.

I see you look at me with startled eyes. In my youth 'twas very common for parents to be loathed rather than loved. Some thoughts still rankle. The Bible tells us we must honour them, but dictatorial ways do not breed affection. I tried to rule with fondness as a mother, rather than through fear. Perhaps I went too far, I know not. I only know I have their love yet, those that remain, and am thankful for it. They are good children to me. And better far than this, they are good Christians and good neighbours, who know their duty to themselves and others.

I was not used kindly in my youth. I would not have children spoilt, but hear them out. How oft, a child demanding why a thing should be, do we retort 'because I tell you so', from lack of patience? Yet what avails it, either at home or in the larger state, if children but obey because they must? They should learn to judge betwixt good and evil, or 'twixt lesser ills, else, when they are come to man's estate, how will they live as worthy citizens? Authority must rule, but do it patiently, seeking to guide rather than lead by force. Children will err from time to time, as men do also, and may learn from it, if kindly led. But getting wisdom is no easy matter, and no man has it all, for all occasions.

I question not my father's greater knowledge, only his way of dealing with the lesser sort. He might have made much of us, with more kindness. I doubt not I should have grown under his tutelage, more than his scorn. Why, we had a servant once, simple in his faith and much given to visiting conventicles, where he was told such truths as made my father mock him. He would not stoop to argue with the man in such a way as he might understand, but rather took delight in hearing words he knew to be but foolishness and silly superstition. Whereupon the servant, wounded in his faith, did leave my father's service.

Sir, this is no way to win the lesser sort, either to love us or to bring about a second Paradise. Those with greater learning must seek to raise the ignorant, else we shall never see a better world. But do it tenderly, and not with scorn. I do not say I might have been the equal of my father, but I would he had sought to lift me to his level, for fondness' sake. I might have loved him then, and he got his reward.

I would he had sought to make me his equal, for assuredly we are such before God. Children must err from time to time, but so do all men. Since our first parents were cast out into the wilderness there is no saying, not with certainty, which is the true path, which the false, and 'tis but by trial and error we can say, and having walked this way before, that it leads to the mire.

But, sir, the box is empty, excepting only this last document, and it concerns my father most nearly. It strikes fear in my heart to look on it, but pride also. Our freedoms are but lent to us, and can as readily be taken away. Dated the thirteenth day of August sixteen sixty, and issued by the Court at Whitehall. You must know of this, the royal proclamation for the apprehension of my father and John Goodwin for treasonable writings.

I have some memory of this, for they were days of dread, and fear, though from a source unknown, is felt throughout a household, blowing like cold air through a draughty door. My father, fearing for his life, had left to go into hiding with friends, I know not where, and servants ruled the house. It should have been a time of carefree laughter, my father being absent, but it was not so. Even my sister Mary was thoughtful in her mien, and chided my childish merriment upon occasion. I was much puzzled by it then, she being so unlike herself. It was as though a brooding presence ruled within the house, which all but I could see.

His books to be burned in public by the common hangman, and no man hereafter to print or sell them. This proclamation was put up around the city. So his fame did turn to infamy, the king being restored by general consent, and my father's life was threatened, or so it seemed. Men prize him now for literary merit, but books have higher ends and words more weight than niceties of verse and fancy phrases. In peaceful times as now, when gentlemen of leisure amuse themselves with literary arts and think themselves heroic in composing heroic couplets, 'tis easy to forget that other men, in other times and places, do take such words in earnest and will act upon them.

The Scriptures now are thought mere tales to amuse an idle hour, at best a sort of poetry to instruct us, at worst dismissed as ancient superstition. My father thought not so, nor did he think his task in life was merely to divert his readers. I think this fearsome document does honour him, placarded as it was all over London, and printed in the newspapers of the time. It shows that books are not mere toys, but things of weight and meaning by which we stand or fall, as fortune wills.

Here it speaks of wicked and traitorous principles dispersed in his books. I would not have you think me disobedient to the state, or in favour of forceful overturning of rightful government. No doubt 'twas just, my father should receive some punishment, and see his pamphlets burned. 'Tis but a trifle when others lost their heads. I only mean to say I take some pride in that my father wrote not merely to be crowned with laurel wreaths, commended by his peers and held in honour, but to bring about a better state for men and for the world. If he was mistaken in means, not ends, he stood by what he thought and wrote accordingly.

I know not who preserved this paper amongst these others, but 'tis strange to see it now, a dark reminder of troubled days. A time of terror for those who had thought their freedoms won, not for an interim betwixt oppressions, but for all time. The righteous are apt to think thus.

Yet my father had friends of influence who worked in his behalf. In this he was fortunate. Indeed, I have heard it said that all this placarding about the town to bring him in was but a ruse to get him off the hook and set him free. For all those not named as traitors in the Act of Indemnity, which was debated round about this time, could not thereafter be charged with any offence against the late king or his government. So a false hue and cry was set in motion for his arrest to excuse his name not being listed in the Act which, once made law, the indictment set against him was null and void.

I know not if this be so, and none, I think, can say with certainty. But that fear did stalk his days and nights about this time is sure. For though the immediate peril might be past, yet did my father dread that some fanatic, angered at his escape from execution, might do the deed himself. He lay awake at nights, and kept himself as private as he could, fearing to walk abroad.

It had been easily done, being blind and elderly, though none attempted it. For though the government was politic, wishing more to reconcile than set asunder, the mob is otherwise, its fury terrifying. Of this I have some knowledge, and speak not from hearsay.

About this time we moved to Holborn, and it was down this street, but shortly after, that I saw from our windows how the howling mob did bear the corpses, lately disinterred, of Cromwell, Bradshaw and of Ireton, to be hung at Tyburn. This is a sight, sir, that is with me yet, more so the sounds, for the very walls did seem to shake and tremble. I screamed with terror, and my sisters took me from the windows to a back room, tried to stop my ears, and sang to me some childish songs, so I would cease to hear. But I heard it still, and sobbed with fright, and would not be consoled. Then came our governess and made us pray upon our knees until the noise abated.

My father? He was all this time within his study, and made no sound. He would tap upon the walls, or rap the floor when help was needed, yet we heard him not. 'Tis little wonder, you may say, in such commotion. But our ears were accustomed to hear his least command, sleeping or waking, during night or day. Had he been present, I think I would remember, since every image of that dreadful day is etched upon my mind, and will be till my death.

Our governess did calm us with her words. Pray to God, she told us, not to aid you, but to cast out fear. And praying did so, I think, for hearing our own words spoken out loud in unison did calm our racing hearts and stop our ears to other noises.

I know not who kept this proclamation, but 'tis a dark memento, fearful in its import. I will not let it go from me, though you ask for it. I would have my children look on it, and bear it in their minds. Though they are poor, his blood runs in their veins for all that. If thoughts are free, expression bears a price when authors stray too far from those who read them, or hold them in contempt. Think you not so? My father found this out.

If 'twas he kept this paper, then it was from pride and not contrition, of that you may be sure. Pride in him was strong. It was a dreadful time. But he was privileged, as other men were not, having friends to hide him, and plead his cause amongst the powerful, and see that he came to no harm. He neither lost his life nor fled abroad, as others did, and though he was detained some little time in prison he was soon released, and was greatly honoured in his last years. 'Tis not ever thus, and men of humbler origin, though with as great a vision, have suffered much, with no man to defend them.

Let me close the box. I hope you have got some profit from it, if not in coin. And though you go with empty hands, your head has more in it now than when you came. You are welcome to such homespun thoughts and patchwork recollections as I am mistress of, I can give you little else for your trouble in coming here. We are poor, and but rich in memories. Now I must to my daughter, so pray excuse me.

FIVE

OUR FATHER WHICH art in Heaven, hallowed be Thy name. Thy kingdom come. Thy will be done, in earth as it is in Heaven. Teach us to know Thy will, Father, so we may follow it, whether to act in righteousness, or suffer meekly if need be, and seek no comfort in this life except in Thee. Teach us to know, Father, when we should be the instruments of Thy commands, and hear Thy voice, and when it is meet for us to bow our heads before the whirlwind of Thy wrath. We are but children, Lord, mere sinners, and many voices speak to us, and seem to come from Thee. Teach us to know Thy will, and know it truly, casting out our own, lest it deceive us, thinking it comes from Thee.

Give us this day our daily bread, and forgive us our trespasses. If I have asked, Lord, more than Thou hast thought fit to give, I humbly beg to be forgiven. There has been bread on the table this night, and for this I thank Thee. It has not been ever thus, and yet Thou hast seen fit to spare me, and bring some comfort to me in this time. Truly the days of miracles are not yet past, that this should be so, and I humbly thank Thee.

Forgive me, Lord, for I confess that fear is ever in my heart. I know the words, Lord – surely goodness and mercy shall follow me all the days of my life.

And yet, Father, I am but a weak vessel. In my youth I had great dread in my heart, that my children should be taken from me. When Thou didst take them to Thyself I grieved and wept. Though our faith teaches us to rejoice, I could not do so. And now, being an old woman, I fear for those children you have left me, those two of the ten I bore in sorrow, Urban and Elizabeth, to be a comfort to me in my old age. Their life is hard, Father, and like to continue so.

I pray, Father, for my son Urban, that he may find a good wife, and prosper at his trade. Also for my daughter Elizabeth, much cast down of late by the death of her newborn child, and in poor health. Bring her to term, and with a living child, and let them prosper, for times are as hard now as they were when my husband yet lived, and uncertain still.

Thy kingdom come. These words Thy son did teach us, to repeat from day to day. In my youth, Father, we thought that day must surely come, and we should live to see it here on earth. I am old now, and my time is spent. Soon I shall be in Thy glory. Yet my offspring suffer, and lack all hope of better days to come. Must it be so, Father? Is it not given to us to bring about a second Paradise in this world, as was hoped for in my father's time, and in my husband's?

It grieves me, Father, to see them live as we did, ever uncertain of their daily bread, for all their industry and skill. My husband was diligent in his workshop, yet got little from it but cares, and left his widow naught but penury. His children scarce fare better. There is talk now of giving up the looms and keeping a grocer's shop, or some such business. Thy will be done. Guide them, Lord, for I fear lest they but exchange one heap of troubles for another.

If Mr Clarke were living now it would give him great sorrow to see such long apprenticeships go for nothing. Is it for this they served, to peddle candles or half pounds of lard? Help Thy servants, Lord, for this earth is yet a wilderness. The market rules, and those with skills so dearly learnt must waste them, if they would eat. Be with them, Father, and keep them in Thy grace. And teach our betters who do govern us to legislate in wisdom, for they do little to protect our livelihoods, and count but cheap those skills so dearly bought, which yet must ever be the rock on which our country's wealth is founded.

Teach us to know Thy ways, for we but wander blindly since our first parents were cast out from Eden. We err as humans will, yet do we love Thee, and would live as Christians should. Keep us in charity, lest hardship makes hard hearts. For though we have but little, and oft dread the day to come, I know full well that many in this land do fare far worse than us.

Thy kingdom come, we pray, the better and the lesser sort alike, as Christians were commanded. Yet do beggars roam our streets, crying 'for charity', and are not heard. Is it enough to mumble with our mouths and yet do nothing, attending passively upon His coming, till time runs out maybe, the Jews converting not? For I was taught that Jesus would not come again to rule His kingdom till the earth was worthy to receive Him, and saints, not sinners, ruled. What must we do, dear Lord, to bring about the Second Coming, His kingdom here on earth? Hear our prayer, and open up the hearts of evil men, who listen not to Thee.

There are those, the younger, fashionable sort,

who think that heavenly revelations now are past, and nature runs its course without Thy meddling. Whatever is, is right, is now the watchword, so peasants lose their little patch of ground and starve in city streets, whilst great lords roam the meadows, all their own, and sheep grow fat, and men and women starve. They fence their parks for sport and recreation, reduce their tenants unto beggary, have town and country houses, lavish wealth on ornaments, fine gowns and carriages, yet turn their labourers out of doors to roam the highways, refusing poor relief to those not born within the parish, when the parish of their birth has made them homeless, destroying their poor hovels and their paltry living. They crowd our cities, Lord, sleep out of doors, and shame us with their plight. Yet those whose shame it is are pitiless, and know no shame. They make their parks a pleasing landscape, remove all things displeasing from their view, and when they go abroad they ride within their carriages, and look not out. Their lofty mansions in the town are guarded well by lackeys, so no importunate beggars cross their path, in seeking alms.

Our Father, who sees into all hearts, unto whom all secrets are known, teach them who but pray to Thee with their lips to open their hearts to Thy will, and do Thy work on earth. For such hypocrisy must offend Thee, as it offends all true believers. Teach them to follow Thy commandments, for they do not, though they may go to church on Sunday, and bow their heads in piety. Thou shalt not steal, we say, yet is the land stolen from those who tilled it formerly to fill their bellies. That common treasury, the earth, is taken from the many by the few, and landlords, whom greed makes greedier, would starve their tenants, and hang the needy who dare poach a rabbit for the cooking pot.

And so it is with all the ten commandments. Who loves his neighbour as himself? We kill, and steal, and covet, and call such sins by other names, to justify our ways. Thou shalt have no other gods before me, this was Thy first commandment, yet wealth and property is now the graven image many worship, that should worship Thee.

They call this freedom, Lord, a land of liberty, to take what you can get and let the Devil take the hindmost. And yet, Lord, when Thou didst vouchsafe us freedom, Thou didst give it not to us so we should plunder, but to choose betwixt good and evil. This was the freedom Thou didst see fit to give us, and I fear we choose but evil.

How shall Thy kingdom come, this being so? Open their hearts, I pray, and let Thy love enter in, that we may yet see a world fit for Christ to reign in.

Father, hear Thy humble servant, for there is no help in us.

SIX

Now, CHILDREN, YOU will not be quarrelling amongst yourselves, I hope. Such a commotion I never did hear. The neighbours will be round in a trice, fearing there is murder afoot. Susan, come here this instant, and dry your tears, Liza. No, I will not have arguing neither, of who's right, who's wrong, and who began it. 'Tis all one, and you are both at fault, and must mend your manners. It is a poor thing if those who think themselves friends do bicker over some trifle, and come to blows. For that it was some silly trifle I have no doubt. So come, both of you, and tell me what set you scrapping like mongrels in the gutter.

A piece of ribbon? This little scrap of cloth that will scarce go round your noddle, or tie a bow, or hold a cap in place? For shame, the both of you, to quarrel so for such a little thing, and scratch each other's cheeks, and pull your hair, and ruin your gowns with tearing. What would your parents say, to see you now, who have laboured hard and long to get you fitly clothed? Your stockings torn and twisted, and, if my eyes mistake not, a seam ripped open. Is this the way you show your gratitude, repaying thus their pains?

Bring me my workbox, child, and I will try to mend matters as best I may, else you will get a whipping before nightfall, so I think. Now dry your eyes, I'll hear no ifs and buts, who first began it, who did what, and who was most at fault. The blame lies in you both, and both should be ashamed to act so. As for the ribbon, I will keep it now, so neither of you has it, since you cannot come to terms. No argument, I care not for your quarrels, who's right, who's wrong. 'Tis all one to me. I would have quiet, and the household orderly.

Come now, dry your eyes, and sit beside me whilst I try to tidy you. Your hair is disordered, and all in tangles. Ouch, you may well say ouch, who did it, pray? Sit still, else it will only hurt the more. Pulling your head away will not mend matters, the knots must be undone. You should have thought on this before beginning.

Sit still and I will tell you a story, whilst I set you both to rights. But first you must kiss and make up, for I will not have those who should be friends, and love one another, pull each other by the hair and roll around the floor like a pair of wild wolf cubs. What kind of conduct is that, pray? Did not Jesus tell us to love one another, and live in amity, and share that which we have, however small and poor it be, and is this how you follow his commands? Shame on you both, to make such a pother over a mere trifle. You must learn to settle arguments more peaceably than this, or it will go ill with you when you are grown and have greater cause to fall out with one another.

So, now you are quiet I will tell you a tale of quarrelling, and what happens to those who must be ever arguing amongst each other, when they should be making common cause to save themselves. For flocks of sheep should huddle close together, and baah and bleat to keep the wolf at bay, not stray far off from pen and from the herd, where they are easy prey. For there is strength in numbers for the weak, if they but act in concord. But falling out and straying, the wolf will have his dinner sure enough.

Once upon a time, when I was but a little girl like you, there was a mighty shepherd to his flock, who kept the wolf at bay. He had been a soldier, fought in many battles, and could marshal silly sheep for their protection, so they did not stray too far, or fall down cliffs or into gullies, nor were swept away by running water. As for the wolves, he knew them well, and built his fences high, drove them far off with barking dogs, with loud and frightening noises, and ever kept a musket by his side. The leader of the pack, the king of wolves, he had long since shot dead and chopped his head off.

Whilst he lived, his sheep felt mostly safe, though they misliked him. Many felt unfree, for being closely penned and herded up together, they could not wander off at will to taste the tempting grass of sweeter meadows, and pasture as they pleased. Why did you kill the king of wolves, they'd bleat, if now we cannot wander as we please over hill and meadow, without your dogs go snapping at our heels, to round us up? Is this what you call freedom?

Yet this shepherd, who had been a soldier, knew what his sheep did not – that troops must march together to withstand the enemy, and make common cause. And I tell you this, he hated nothing so much in this world as squabbling and petty arguments, and had he seen the two of you just now, he would have knocked your heads together, and sent you supperless to bed. He has done as much to grown men, and sent them packing when they could not be of one mind.

But no man lives for ever, and no thing is done for good and all. Weeds grow in tidy gardens, as they say. The shepherd died at last, as all men must, and left his flock to his son Richard, who was quite another sort of man, kindly but undecided. When his sheep did wander off in all directions he knew not what to do, as some roamed east, and others west, some north, a couple south, and none obeyed his whistles and his shouts. Why should we heed his cries, the sheep did bleat, we fear him not. Besides, the king of wolves is dead, and cannot harm us. So at last we may enjoy the meadows, freely roam, and follow our desires.

But, alas, my children, these were silly sheep, to think thus. For though the old wolf king was dead, yet he had many followers in the pack, who gnashed their teeth with glee at seeing such foolish conduct, both the straying sheep and their weak shepherd, lacking authority and strength of purpose. Why, even his dogs would not obey him, but charged about at will, chasing the sheep hither and thither as the mood took them, thinking themselves the shepherd, that should be but his tool. For dogs are swift of foot, their teeth do bite, yet is their task but to obey, not to take command.

Besides, although the old wolf king was dead, he too had had a cub, now grown large and strong, who prowled beyond the gates, and paced the fences, and bided but his time to gobble up the flock. Indeed, it seemed that even Heaven knew that the old shepherd's passing did bode no good, for on the night he breathed his last a great storm such as the land had not witnessed in living memory blew across the countryside, lifting off roofs and chimneys, felling trees as though with a vast windy axe, knocking down walls and fences, and tumbling poor fishermen from out their tossing boats.

It was such a storm, my children, as none within the kingdom could recall, and indeed, though I was but a child, I yet remember the terror of those hours, how I did tremble beneath the sheets, hearing the windows rattle, shutters bang, and an eerie screech wail round the chimney pots and moan within the house like some unhappy ghost. I clung to my big sister in a fright, so she should comfort me, and hold me tight. And in the morning, going down below, our old servant said she had not slept a wink, and swore it was a sign of great events now ending, or yet to come, and boded ill, being surely Heaven's wrath at sins committed. Which made me wonder much that God should know my little peccadillo of the day before, and make such great commotion in His anger. So guilt will find us out, as you well know, my children, and I had stolen cakes from out the kitchen the previous night.

It was not a day like other days. The streets were empty, but for bits of branches that tossed and tumbled, and no one stirred abroad. And all men knew that Cromwell now was dying, our Lord Protector. I still recall the feelings of those hours, the bolted doors that rattled, and the howling gale about the house. There was an awesome silence within doors, despite the storm, or on account of it. A sense of waiting for it to subside, but fear was in the air, I felt it, for all my youth. I never saw such praying within doors, neither before nor since, except when my first stepmother did die some months before. Thus I knew that death was in the air, though none within our house was sick. Besides, my stepmother had died in quietness, her infant also. This was otherwise. It was as though the whole world was being tossed and turned, and all must suffer.

When the storm subsided I saw our garden wrecked. We had a pretty garden at that time where I could play in summer, and my father sat. Beyond it lay the park, St James's, and there so many trees were felled, their roots up in the air, as though some fearsome giant stalked the earth, destroying as he went. I scarce believed my eyes, to look upon such havoc, and my eyes can see it yet, as clear as yesterday, though I was but a child as you are now, and many, many sights which I have seen since then have left no trace behind.

No sooner was the Lord Protector dead, than those who had been too fearful in his lifetime to argue and to quarrel on how the kingdom should be governed, set to again. Instead of thinking on the enemy without the gates, they sought but enemies within, and therein lay their downfall. Divide and rule, this is an ancient maxim they too easily forgot, and were defeated by it.

Two factions quickly rose, that which would keep the government as it had been but lately constituted, with Richard at its head; and the Army party who, thinking the cause for which they fought now long betrayed, would have all things ordered anew. Like sheepdogs, their old master dying, they turned on his weakling son. We did the shepherd's work for him, they barked, now we shall herd the flock. We know best where they should pasture, and will not heed his whistle.

So all the chief dogs did meet together and decided that they would not have this shepherd Richard for their master. They had feared his father, and obeyed him to the end, but his son was not so fierce, and lacked authority. So when they barked at him, and told him go, he went without a murmur, fearing their teeth, and having little stomach for a fight. Having no will of his own, he saw the will of God in all things, and was much unlike his father in this, who found rather his will to be the Lord's. Whether it is more Christian to be resigned, or fight for Christian virtues, I scarcely know. Either way, I fear, we may end up with the Devil.

Sit quiet, children, you must hear me out. The tale is not yet told. So now, the shepherd's son being chased from out the farmhouse, this pack of dogs, the army officers, could choose to herd their flock as they thought fit. But how? That was the question more readily posed than answered. For each dog had his opinion, and barked as loudly as he could to make it heard. Such a commotion, children, never yet was heard. The birds were frighted off, and left their nests, and hens mislaid their eggs.

You laugh, my dears, to hear me tell it so, but truly, 'twas no laughing matter. For I fear these dogs, like all men of good will the whole world over, are ever more united on that which they would banish, than on those things with which they would replace it. So it was now. Each dog would have his say, and thought himself the best for barking loudest. Since all did bark, none listened, nor could they, for so much noise.

At long last they all grew tired of this confusion, put down their heads between their paws, and slept soundly through the night. Next morning they decided that each should bark in turn, and give their views on governing the sheep. So it was done. The first dog gave it as his opinion, that a council should be held each morning, and a vote taken, as to where the sheep should graze. Another thought that going by rotation, with each dog taking turns to have his day, would be a wiser course. These two proposals resulted in some scrapping between the rival camps. The noise grew loud, until an aged dog, silent until that time, proposed a compromise. Each dog should have his day, but that the common council should have the right of veto. Or, if you prefer, the common council should be held each day, but that two senior dogs should have the right of veto. Either way, a balance would be struck.

These notions much impressed all those who listened, yet could they not decide on which course to follow, the problem being this. Whichever course they chose as being the most just, it must be justly chosen. One vote for each, squeaked out a lively puppy, wagging his tail. But all those present barked out their objections, and drowned him out.

When the uproar had grown less a black dog with a patch of white across one eye proposed that each dog should have as many votes as he had years, thus giving each a voice but also due weight to seniority and wisdom. No fool like an old fool, squeaked the puppy, but was bitten in the ear and withdrew to whimper most piteously. The young one being silenced, and the bitch who bore him told that females have no vote, this method found much favour with the majority.

Now quite tired out with so much hot debate, the sun being set, the dogs all slept again. But the following morning new disputes arose. One had dreamed, for dogs do dream, that the Good Shepherd of ancient lore was come to earth again, and thought they all should hold themselves in readiness for Him, not outlaw single rule. It was time, they all agreed, to vote upon the method of procedure. But the problem now was this: should each dog have one vote to vote upon the voting, or several votes according to his age?

This caused a new commotion, for if they voted each according to his age, then the procedure which they sought to choose, it was already chosen. But if by simple vote, it was not valid, whether passing or defeated. For if defeated, it was by a method neither just nor chosen, if passed, then by a method now rejected.

Besides, said one, a genius at mathematics, there is a bias either way. For if we vote with one voice each, it is but natural that the younger dogs will vote against the other method, it being unfavourable to them. But if each have a vote according to their age, the outcome is foregone. Why, our oldest member is nigh on fifteen years, and can outvote us all, or almost. Sixteen, growled the dog, which began a scuffle, for several said he lied.

Thus passed another day in argument, for none did rightly know how to proceed to reach agreement. To complicate the case no dog could prove his age beyond all doubt, their births being not recorded in a book. Besides, they could not read. A shaggy mongrel limping on three legs proposed that, length of years going with infirmity, those with least teeth and most grey hairs should have most say, these being signs of venerable status. But this found little favour with the pack, since herding sheep requires authority, and barking without bite is little use.

The sun being long since set, they took their rest, and slept most soundly, wearied with their labour. They woke to hear a twittering of birds upon the rooftop, and hens a-cackling in the yard, the cockerel crowing lustily, and all the feathered kind, it seemed, likewise engaged in arguing how nature should be run. A wondrous chorus rose unto the morning sky, a sweet cacophony of sound, heralding freedom's dawn. It was a very parliament of fowls, shrill and disorderly. The cock crowed loudest, boasting how, alone of all the birds, he made the sun to rise, but lesser voices drowned him with their squabbles.

The dogs rose up, and prowled about the yard, but no bird paid them heed. Small sparrows picked the ground afront their paws, then flew aloft at will. Hens left the farmyard, heedless of the rooster, and laid their eggs in hedgerows far from home, whilst fluttering doves cooed round their cote.

The dogs yawned, stretched, and broke their fast, then settled down to work. A thought had come to one of them, which, until then, had not been voiced. He put it forward now as but a thought, with some timidity. Shall we consult the sheep? It being for their welfare that we labour, would it not help us in our work if they ran willingly where we would lead them?

This was a novel notion, and as such must needs be much discussed from each and every angle. It being known that sheep were silly, with but little brain, it was not meet to ask for their opinion unless the outcome was assured. For sheep, 'twas known, would wander into gullies, be swept away by floods, or eat such crops as were not meant for them, and which could do them harm. Left to their own devices, all agreed, the flock will perish, or we lose them every one. This being so, the choice, such as we give them, must be no choice at all.

So, said the eldest dog, what we must do is to put to them but those questions where the answers matter not a jot. We must not ask them whither they would roam, or when move on. These are weighty matters, only fit for us. Ask not whether they would graze upon the upper or the lower meadow, but tell them they must go into the lower meadow, choosing the gate by which they enter, the lefthand or the right. Likewise it matters not to us which sheep goes first, and which shall follow after, provided all go in. Leave to them the order of their going, as being but their democratic right, and they will sheeplike follow our commands, and make our task far easier than till now.

In all this time they quite forgot their sheep. For while they talked and argued, point by point, their flock had wandered off, being long since unattended, and hungry for new pasture. They bleated first, but when none heard their cries one of them found a gate left loose and pushed it open. The whole flock followed, and soon they strayed, this way and that across the hillside, for juicy grass, sweet clover and the like. For sheep must graze or starve, this being nature's way, and stomachs will not wait, as you well know.

At first they wandered idly, following their nose for choicest feeding. But as night drew on the beasts grew fearful, finding their numbers scattered far from home, with neither dog nor shepherd to protect them. Lost now in ones and twos in darkest night, the shadows boded ill, each eerie sound might be a beast of prey stalking the night to kill them. They huddled in their pelts beneath thorn hedges, or in dips and hollows, and prayed for daylight.

When the dawn was come they found but little comfort. Far from home, under a wintry sky, they bleated piteously to find each other, the flock being scattered over hill and dale. Neither did they know the best way to proceed, being used so long to obey their shepherd and his snarling dogs.

And so they strayed, hither and thither, through unknown fields and meadows, knowing not which way to go. Until at last some few of them did find a neighbouring farmhouse, and upon the stoop a sheepdog, fast asleep. They woke him with their cries and pleaded with him to find their fellow sheep. For we are lost, they said, and have no shepherd, and singly we will perish.

This was a wise old dog, who barked but little, and heard them out. Some called him cunning and, if cunning is to bark but little and prick up your ears to hear the sounds around you, he was so. His name was George, and in the farmyard he was oft called Silent George, being seldom heard to bark, a quality but rarely found in dogs.

Being silent, and but wagging of his tail, this dog did hear them out, those silly straying sheep. Please help us, they did bleat, for we have strayed and know not our way home. The flock is scattered, round us up, we pray.

The dog did nod most sagely, heard their pleas, then trotted off abroad, through field and meadow. No path was left untrod, no common ground left unexplored. Little by little he did round them up, the forlorn, bedraggled flock. Some were found huddled in the lea of rocky boulders, others wandering through woods or on the highway. One old sheep was caught in midstream, trying to cross the water, and knew not whither. Their fleeces snagged with burs, some lame of foot, they followed where his snout did usher them, this wily dog. And so they ran before him, glad to be a flock once more, in which they found much comfort. For to be singly straying through the land could do them naught but harm.

And so he brought them home, this wily dog, not to the home they left, but to his master's, who praised him highly and rewarded him with titbits. The sheep cared little who was now their master, being weary and despondent. After such little liberty as they had savoured they feared but anarchy, and would no longer roam unshepherded. To be forever herded in a flock was their delight, and if this master had an appetite for mutton pie, they bore it humbly, hoping the axe would fall upon some other neck than theirs, they going unnoticed in the herd.

Meanwhile the several sheepdogs at the other farm were arguing yet, how best to herd their sheep, when one of them, returning from a walk abroad, informed them that the flock had vanished quite, the pasture empty and the fields around deserted likewise. On hearing which the dogs got in a frenzy and began to search the country all around, scampering about the hillsides in despair.

They found no sheep, and when at last they found a flock with other markings grazing in a field, the boy who watched the herd threw stones at them, then fetched his master, who, to send them off, did fire his musket. One dog was hit and died, the rest ran off, to skulk within the woods like wolves or foxes, fearing the hunt. And so they lived out miserable lives, outcast, in hiding, who had sought to guide the flock, and lead it to green pastures presently, dissension being ended. Had their argument been less they might have kept their sheep, and lived out lives of honour, not contempt.

This, my little ones, was a tale told to me in my childhood, against quarrelling by those that should be friends. Mind it well, such fables come from truth, and should instruct us. Well may you weep, as I shed tears to hear it, as did the teller who first told it me. But wipe your eyes, for tears will not mend matters. Kiss and make up, you two that should be friends, for out of doors are enemies enough, who wish you ill. Now to supper, for it grows late.

SEVEN

YOU COME TO a grieving household, sir. I fear you find us much cast down in spirit. It is but two days since we buried her, who should have seen us put into the ground. But eight years old, and as healthy a child as you could wish to see a month ago. I can scarce credit it even now, though I have had much sorrow in my time. I bore ten infants, to bury seven before they were out the cradle. Alas, sir, old age takes many pleasures from us, but not our sorrows. I had not thought to feel such grief again, but yet I feel it nearly.

Eight years old, sir, and such a child as would make your heart glad. Pretty as a picture, and as lively as a cricket but a month since. If you had heard her then, how she would chatter, and run laughing down the alley, you would not have thought it possible. No, sir, pray stay. We must master what we cannot help. I must ask you to forgive my woman's frailty, which now overcomes me. I had not thought to weep in strangers' company, and beg your pardon.

Have you brought books to try me? I will dry my eyes, and you may test me. Yet I fear my eyes are weak now, and I see but poorly. Else I might yet have earned a little by my teaching, lessening the burden which I now must be upon my daughter's household. They have so little that I would not make it less. Yet am I thankful to have a living child to care for me, being old. It is a comfort for which I thank God daily. Else had I died long since, of want, and lack of love. To bury many children is a sorrow which a man can never know, having borne them not, flesh of his flesh, in living anguish. Though his heart may grieve, he finds much comfort in other labours and, if his wife should die in childbed, takes another, to give him living heirs. His grief is milder, and his loss but temporary, finding new rewards on earth, which we must seek in Heaven.

I fear now for my daughter, suffering this loss. She has buried two babes already, that were born sickly. Now this, our little Liza. Who would have thought it, so full of life, and never ailing till now. For eight long years she thrived, and scarcely gave us cause to feel anxiety, though every mother is anxious from time to time, when fever comes, or cold, or babes grow fretful. 'Tis but natural, part of our daily care. This we bear gladly, finding our reward in thriving children who grow strong and tall. But such a loss as this, how can we bear it? She says but little, sir, yet I do fear the grief is deeper for it. I wish she would weep, as I do, and give release to that which burdens her. For to be sparing in our tears is to be heavier yet of heart, carrying the burden longer.

And she carries another burden within her, which grows with every month. They say a woman should not weep when with child, else it will know but sorrow. I would have a son, she told me but yesterday, for I would not have a child of mine, if it should live, feel what I feel this day. This she said to me, her face so stony and her cheeks so pale, you might have thought her dead to all the world. But I know otherwise, for I have been where she dwells now, and my heart breaks for her, a second rupture, doubling my grief. I would I could give her ease, both for herself and for the child that grows within her. We pray both night and morning, but as yet the words rise easier than our hearts.

The Lord giveth and the Lord taketh away, and we must bear our grief as best we may. Truly, we are punished most bitterly for the sin of our first mother, in eating of that tree. Yet I cannot think that, when He takes unto Himself such little ones as our sweet Liza, He does it out of wrath against our fallen race, but rather out of love for such dear innocence. Think you not so?

But you did not come for this. Please do not seek to leave, sir, it is I who am at fault in going on so. What cannot be cured must be endured, as the saying goes, and it may ease my mind to speak of other matters.

So, what would you know of me? Have you brought ancient texts for me to read out loud, in Greek or Hebrew? I will do it gladly, can I but find my spectacles. I have done it oft before, when learned gentlemen did visit me. I think, sir, they would have proved me and my sisters liars, that would calumniate our father out of hate and bitterness. You do protest, but I fear 'tis so, women being oft thought tellers of untruth by very nature, sinning most when telling tales of our most sainted men, whom history reveres. My father now is such, and so they would not think him cruel to his daughters. Come, sir, you came to test me, is it not so? You need not blush, I take it not unkindly, and I will read your Greek for you, if you have it by you, and my eyes fail me not.

But I am no liar, and would I had happier memories of my youth, and fonder tales to tell you. It gives me naught but grief to speak ill of a father long since forgiven. Besides, such stories as you hear come not from me but from my cousin Edward, who knew our household as did no other man, loved my father most tenderly, and revered his work. Would he besmirch his idol, except to honour truth? It was but lately the great world knew I lived, a lowly widow, poor and in distress. Since then I do confirm what has been told, and do it sadly, no more. I think fondly now of him who fathered me, pitying his faults. For is it not a matter for great pity, that a man should find no love within his heart for offspring given him by God? Had I three daughters now to comfort me I would thank my Maker from my heart. Mine He took, all but Elizabeth, as Liza now is taken.

He had a son, sir, taken in infancy. Did you know this? I think that had he lived, he might have lavished on him such fondness as he did not show to us, being but girls. Women are our misfortune, he would say, and liked to tell me in his mocking fashion that Eve was Adam's rib, and his misfortune, the word in Hebrew meaning both at once. *Tsela* the word is, if my memory serves me right. You see the limits of my scholarship, a thorn but meant to goad us. Such academic niceties did much delight him, for he would use superior scholarship to humble those beneath him, such as us, not raise us up.

I have no recollection of this brother, for he died shortly after my birth, which took my mother. And yet his little life did haunt our household in later years, like unto a promise given but not fulfilled. A nurse was blamed for his untimely death, whilst I, the newborn infant, thrived. He had borne it better, so I think, if I had been the child to perish, and my brother lived. The nurse, dismissed, had now become an ogress, though our old servant spoke of her as blameless in the matter, and much maligned.

The Lord giveth, and the Lord taketh away, and we must bear such griefs in all humility. To do otherwise is but to prolong our anguish, and blind us to His mercy, which is a mystery we cannot fathom. This is a teaching of our faith which I have clung to, through many such times of loss, and their attendant pain. Yet I fear humility was not my father's forte, or his chiefest virtue, but he must ever blame some faulty woman when things did go awry, despite our best endeavour. I think he thought that God would do his bidding, did he but follow virtue, as he saw it, and so must blame some weaker vessel when misfortune struck. The Book of Job was not for him, there being no woman in the case.

You smile, sir, but indeed it is no smiling matter if born to petticoats. It is no light thing, ever to bear the sins of man upon slight shoulders, shrug them as you may, they drop not off. Christ our Saviour died to take our sins from us, both men and women, yet for my father, in his deepest heart, woman was not redeemed, and bore the sins of Eve, and many since, her nature being more fallible.

I am old now, and think that we must bear that which we cannot alter, nor seek to question it this side the grave. Our little Liza's gone, and there's an end, and no theology will bring her back, nor reasoning restore her. Who then should I blame for this our sorrow, to make it less? What balm is anger to a gaping wound, to close it up? I think, sir, we must rather be as little children are, accepting humbly what we cannot understand, and trusting in His mercy. This was not my father's way, else had he lived a more contented man, instead of pouring scorn on lesser men, whether in skirts or breeches. Harsh words, I know, but I am grown too old to mince matters for a stranger.

So, you have brought no texts for me to read? I confess I am glad of it, my eyesight being so poor. They say I look much like him, and Mr Addison was pleased to say, when I first met him, that I did need no other voucher, my face being testimonial enough of whose daughter I had been. Weak eyes are yet another, one I could rather do without.

His eyesight being gone when I was born, he never saw me. Is this not strange? I thought it so. And nursed the notion, had he but known my face and how like it was to his, he might have loved me better. Yet I fear the wish was father to an idle thought, since he cared little for my sisters, whom he had seen at first. I think he saw our mother in us, and liked us less for it.

Well, sir, we must bear that which we cannot alter. There are those who say that all we suffer is a punishment for sin, and none is without sin. They said this of my father, he being struck blind so soon after the king was executed, and he defending it. I see you look aghast, but these are other times, less superstitious, and more prone to look for natural causes in unusual events. Why, sir, did you know that when General Monck did march from up north to London, there were those who saw in this the prophecy of Daniel come to pass? I jest not, nor did my father jest in having Satan raise his standard in the north. The words go thus – So the king of the north shall come, and cast up a mount, and take the most fenced cities: and the arms of the south shall not withstand, neither his chosen people, neither shall there be any strength to withstand.

Know you the passage? It is not the custom now, I know, to read the Bible as was done formerly, in my youth. It comes from Daniel. A book much favoured at that time for prophecy. Why, sir, when silent George – I mean the General Monck – did march from north to south, the most ignorant apprentice could have told you that passage, and discoursed upon its meaning, and others similar. We knew our Bible, sir, and saw in it a map for past and future, that should guide us on a way that none had trod before. My late husband did read it so, being persuaded in his youth that Daniel told us the Second Coming was at hand.

Do not mock us, sir, for I see something of laughter in your eye. How else should they proceed, but by the Book, in such a wilderness? If you have come here out of reverence for my father, you must not mock, for he, like other men, did think thus. Why, even Cromwell and his officers did halt their counsels for to hear a prophetess who came to speak with them, so think it not confined to lesser men, the meaner sort, unschooled and unrefined. No, we lived by the Book, aye, lived and died for it, most often.

Now I am old I see it otherwise, as do my children, born in another time, with lesser hopes. Indeed, I know that I was born too late to feel the full force of the hope that moved my father's time, and spurred them on. I have but heard the echoes of that epoch, muted by disenchantment, and from persons long since disabused, their faith embittered. You are younger far than I, and cannot know the age of which I speak. Whether you are in this more fortunate, I know not. Is it better in this world to have our hopes deferred, and shattered utterly, or to be born without? For you, sir, being born to wealth, such questions have but little meaning. Indeed, that things should long continue as they are must be your comfort, rather than your pain. For the poor 'tis otherwise.

As for General Monck, he was by some called a wolf in sheep's clothing, that did betray us at the last, and we the helpless flock. I have some recollection of that time, vivid yet, the days being so tumultuous. His name was on all lips, whilst turmoil reigned without upon the streets. What would he do, what not, his troops now drawing near, like to a vengeful messenger of God, or mystery of fate, I know not which. Being but a child, with a child's fancy, his name for me did conjure up some fearful ogre, with the power to blow down chimney stacks at will, and gobble naughty children for his supper.

Fear and excitement both, a sense of awe, and great events in train. This was the feeling as the army marched towards us. All tongues a-wagging, and the streets unruly, wellnigh to anarchy. Groups of apprentices did roam about the town, jeering at soldiers, or pelting them with stones. The military scarce dared show their faces in the city, for fear of angry citizens, and streets chained off, and all men crying for a free parliament, not the ancient Rump but lately re-assembled.

I saw then with the eyes of a child. Now I am grown, I know it was not some all-seeing fate, some instrument of God that marched on London, but a man much like any other, uncertain of his path. Nay, with more humility than those he lately served. An instrument of government, and not of God, was how he saw himself, and rather sought to serve the people than to be their master. He

119

listened much, spoke little, and was nicknamed silent George. He heard the people who petitioned him as he marched southward, all calling for a full and free parliament, heard them out, and kept his own counsel. Even my father, as I think you know, did write to him, though in another manner, wishing to avert, even now, what all men wished for.

I think he was much mocked for publishing a pamphlet at that time, which he did send to the General, in which he put forth a ready and easy way to keep the commonwealth, and stop the monarchy from coming back. Alas, had it been so easy, it should have been accomplished long since, and now it was too late. And yet, sir, though he dreamed still when others long had woken, I find in this a kind of hardiness that makes me love him, though I loved him not when I was at his mercy, and a child. I have heard this spoken of with much derision, as showing him to be not merely blind in body, but blind to simple truth. There was a tract published against him, I know, for my cousin showed it me, called *No Blind Guides*, and with the motto, 'If the blind lead the blind, both shall fall into the ditch'.

I have it not, else I would show it you, but it has stayed with me. For my father, you must know, when many saw his blindness as a punishment from God, saw in it a mark of special favour. For God gave poets, like seers, an inner light to see by, whilst lesser men are blind to vision, so he thought.

I do not know if there be truth in this, though Homer too was blind, or so they say. As a child, and ever since, I have thought it marvellous that he should see such things as Paradise, and Heaven, and beauteous Eve, when I saw puddles in a muddy yard, and chilblained hands, and greasy pots that must be scoured. And yet, sir, whether it be a welcome gift to see such visions, turned blind to common things, I still must doubt. The likes of you and me must live in the world as it is, and make do with what we find. If we can discover a little beauty now and then, in a world long since grown ugly, it must suffice us. For we are fallen too far.

Perhaps we are blinded by the common day, as he would have it. But in common justice it is hard to see so far when we are cold and hungry, and want the wherewithal for living decently. I have heard my children crying, not the angels sing. So the hungry man sees puddings in his dreams, and his visions are all of a little comfort, no more than this. But anarchy brings neither, as my uncle was wont to say, no coals to empty hearths, nor cabbages to market.

My father's brother was a royalist, and thought it mighty strange that, in a last ditch stand against the Restoration, some would rather see a commoner made king than rightful Stuart kings returned. But General Monck declined the offer made to him, not from cunning, or devious designs, as many claimed in after years, but that he would in all things abide by his own precept, that a soldier is but an arm of civil government, obeying its commands, never his own desires.

This is a simple thing to do in settled times, but in a time of anarchy and overturning it is not so. For though the House, being then the only voice of government, did order him to put down riots and disorders in the city, the citizens were of another mind, it being not elected recently, but stale with twenty years, nor full and free, so many members being yet excluded.

I think, sir, this must be the hardest thing of all, to go, not with our inclination, but with the will of

God, and men. We women know this sorrow, when our life's labour, in a little child, is taken from us, and we must not question why, but silently accept it. Men that do labour in the world must see their best endeavours come to nought, and suffer it, and take the consequence. Who knows, sir, what he thought, this General, caught as he was betwixt a running tide and principles held dear for many years? And so he first obeyed the Parliament, and quelled the riots. A deed which stupefied all citizens, as I remember, as posts and chains were taken off, and gates unhinged and smashed. Gossip had it that the very soldiers raged to do such work, being loath to do it.

And then his mind was changed and, changing with it, his orders countermanded. Soldiers and citizens were now as one. The bells rang out, housewives gave food and drink to soldiers standing guard, and many a bonfire burnt its rump upon the street, to mark its ending. The Roasting of the Rump, they called it, and apprentices did dance in triumph. Out of doors, sir, was so much joy, such wild rejoicing as it was rare to see, but within hushed voices, an uneasy stillness reigned, like death. We had heard the cheering crowds, the loud huzzahs, as the troops were marched down Whitehall and the secluded members escorted under guard into the House, and though I was but young I understood that something was afoot the like of which I had not known till then. Nor such feelings of division, uncertainty, where evil was, where good.

This I chiefly now remember, not the cheering crowds, the bonfires, and the like, but my perplexity, at such division, that light was dark, dark light, and grown men living under God were so divided.

It was the earliest inkling to my childish mind that eating from the tree by our first parents, though bringing to us knowledge of both good and evil, brought us not sufficient insight to tell us which was which on all occasions.

The certainty that reigned within our house but fuelled my unease. For if my father, this old, blind man, had purchased truth with loss of sight, with learning, then how could God permit such a vast multitude to be deceived, and hurry to their doom with such rejoicing? For so it seemed, I being made to feel that dark days were upon us, and yet the people cheered out on the streets. Was this some living nightmare or a punishment from God for heinous sins committed, and by whom? I did not know, but only felt the world a fearsome place, mysterious, not fully understood.

This is another age, and men live now by other certainties. The Bible now is like some ancient tale, told to divert the childhood of our race, but put aside since then. For you the world's a clock that ticks and ticks, even though its owner sleeps, a steady pace that nothing will disturb. But in my father's time, aye, in my husband's also, for he in youth did think so, time's truth and man's destiny were thought to be unfolding to some great triumph and perfected end, Christ's kingdom upon earth, and this great truth was spoken of in Scripture, which prophesied all things. Hence it followed that promises unkept must come from sin.

I am old now, sir, and have seen much sorrow. This latest grief is but one of many in a long life. I fear such certainty, of right, of wrong, makes a harsh master, and one unkind to human frailty, and human need. And then I think they were mistaken, for we must seek to find Heaven within us, rather than here on earth. I cannot think the Lord would punish an entire people, any more than He would punish my poor daughter by taking Liza from us.

But in those distant times men thought that great events were brought about by God, either to reward or punish, or to fulfil prophecy. So my father thought, enraged at lesser men who now returned the king, and by their lack of virtue kept our Lord from coming down to earth, to establish His kingdom in this land. Is it right, he said, that we, the few, should now return to slavery, because the many choose not to be free? Despising common sense, and common goals, which lesser men must look to. I fear in this great men are greatly blind upon occasion. Besides, sir, that which I endured, my sisters also, was it not a kind of slavery, and brought about by him that spoke of freedom? I fear the liberty he spoke of was but for an elected few.

Some thought the nightmare ended, some the dream, but either way great changes were afoot. I have since heard tell that politicians did indeed behave as though a dream had passed and now all men awoke. General Monck having marched the members purged from out the House so many years before, and sent them into Parliament protected by his soldiers, to cheering crowds, the members within now proceeded to their business as though it had been December eleven years ago, the king's head yet upon his shoulders, and all things as they once had been, before the overturning. They finished speaking of things broken off long since, as a grandam nodding by the fire will wake up suddenly, and speak as though her children were yet by her side, that are departed. Or like men at midsummer, bewitched by elves and fairies, who vanish with the sunrise.

You would have me say whether the dream was good or ill? Alas, sir, though my father's daughter, he did not seek to make me his heir. I was taught to make lace, and do embroidery for rich men's coats, to read a little in my mother's tongue with understanding, but my father's many tongues without due comprehension. I was not raised to speak of such lofty matters, and would you now have me put my head above the parapet so you may shoot it off?

I think that those who call themselves elect of God are prone to human error, being human. In this they chiefly err, not to confess it. Obstinacy in a lost cause is but foolhardy. We must consider why the cause was lost, not cling to idle dreams.

I think, sir, if there be punishment for sin committed by a nation, if sins there were during those troubled times, such punishment will come in direct consequence of folly, and not from Heaven. And yet many thought that great afflictions, other than those brought about by kings and politicians upon a suffering populace, were sent from God. I mean the dreadful pestilence, and the fire that followed after.

That something should occur, momentous, unexpected, was widely held, sixteen sixty-six being the Year of the Beast, as given to us in Revelations. 'Here is wisdom. Let him that hath understanding count the number of the beast: for it is the number of a man; and his number is six hundred threescore and six.' The words are with me yet, for as the year approached they were oft quoted, with hope or dread, or mingling of the two, since even greatest faith must have its doubts, and though we may surmise God's purpose, as many did, the manner of its unfolding must ever be a mystery.

I heard much of this from my late husband, and from others of his trade. For many in his family, along with other people in this neighbourhood, had kept within their hearts the promise of the Second Coming, whilst others made their peace with circumstance. Indeed, a youthful cousin of his rallied to the standard at Mile End, when a headstrong, foolish few sought to rise up against the might of Cromwell, and bring about the godly kingdom here below, long since betrayed. He was imprisoned for his pains and yet, a few years later, when the king had been returned, took part in just another such rebellion, inspired by readings and by discourses in Coleman Street, a favourite meeting place for Christian sects, and with this rabble rampaged through the streets, demanding that King Jesus reign instead of Charles. This time he met his death in the fighting that ensued, and many judged him and his fellows foolish, to think to overturn the powers that be by simple violence.

Such fighting was abjured, but not the hope. This I know from Mr Clarke, and others like him, though humbler than my father, much like to him in this, for all lived by the Book, and by their common hope of better things to come. In the Bible they sought promises of change, being impotent for ought but waiting.

So when the pestilence came to this city, it did seem a punishment from God, as many were struck down from hour to hour. Some thought that this was the beginning of destroying Antichrist, and that our Lord was doing now what men had failed to do. If you should deem this cruel, to think that such a plague should come from God, how much more cruel were it to suppose it came without a purpose? Which, I fear, it did, since many saints did perish, to be thrown into a common pit with strangers, and when it passed the world was much as it had been before, except more empty, and destroyed by fire.

Alas, sir, we must not question God's purpose, or His wisdom, in bringing such great suffering to His people. As I have told my daughter, we must not ask the why and wherefore for such dreadful loss, but rather seek to find our comfort in the knowledge of His mercy, and find our peace therein. Suffer the little children to come unto me, Jesus told us. And they are angels now, of light, having gone into His grace. I have seen so many go before, but I think this latest grief is the hardest blow of all. Forgive me. I am old now, and tears come easily, to put me to shame.

And yet we were spared, sir, at the time of the great pestilence. For all the talk of God's punishment, it must be said the Lord dealt kindly with my father, and so gainsaid their judgement. Whilst thousands died, he lived. We fled the city, it is true, and so escaped the worst, yet even in the countryside some died, as I recall. And when the Great Fire swept the city our house near Bunhill Fields was not destroyed, though we could see smoke rising less than half a mile away.

The fire came so close, we had begun to move out books and chattels from the house, as did our neighbours. So many as he had, it would have been no easy task to save them all. My sister, being loath to shift them, said they would make a merry bonfire. She had a sharp tongue, did Mary, and had but little liking for our father's studious habits. I think she thought to be rid of them at last, but was in this disappointed.

My poor sister would speak in this fashion when the mood was on her, which was frequent. Speaking of my father's lack of sight, I have heard her call it a blessing, else he would know his new wife, our stepmother, had a face no better than the hind parts of a cow. He had no eyes, she said, because he would not see, and so was blind. My father, for his part, would say that God had punished him with daughters, unkind, undutiful, and what you will. And so the taunts flew back and forth, ever more barbed, like arrows.

Though she bore her mother's name, and was hated for it, I think Mary was more like her father than either would acknowledge. She had his wits, left unattended and so grown wild, untamed by discipline or proper use, and like him could be satiric and unsparing. One tongue, so he would say, is enough for any woman, and in my sister's he found one too many for his liking.

These are ancient quarrels, and I would not trouble you with them. My poor sisters are long since dead, and I too old to harbour grudges. Though is it any wonder great men cannot fashion a better world, where all shall live in harmony, if their own private household be ever in a state of civil war?

My sister thought his blindness made him foolish, but I rather was of the opinion that it bestowed on him some special gift, in seeing wondrous visions denied to sighted men. Being but a child, I thought, if I could but keep my eyes shut long enough, I too would see them. And so I stumbled in the dark, trying not to peep, when daylight beckoned from under screwed-up lids, and marvels did not come.

You smile, sir, but the young have simple notions, and must find the world out for themselves. What I thought came from God, it derived from books, which we must read but could not understand. Have you brought a text for me to read? Though my eyes are weak now, never of the best even when young. A poor inheritance for one who must stitch for her daily bread. It is close work, sir, and harms the eyes.

I would offer you some slight refreshment, but you find us unprepared for visitors. Indeed, we have been so taken up with sorrow this last week, that such civility has quite gone by the board. Pray, forgive us.

Think you that all things are foretold, and cannot be amended by what we do? Many have thought so, but 'tis a fearsome doctrine. And yet, sir, to think otherwise brings terrors also, and guilt with it. I would not have my daughter wracked with it, to add to all her woe. I speak to her of God's will, as I was taught to do, but I fear she but listens with half an ear.

Grief is deaf, as I know from my own experience. Must you go, sir? I would not drive you hence, but it is difficult to speak of past times, the present being so heavy on us, and I have but little heart for it.

EIGHT

I S THAT YOU, daughter? I must have slept, I think.
You should have woken me ere this. I would not
be idle. The Devil finds work for idle hands, so they
say, but I have ever striven . . . never a moment
. . . shelling peas in the morning sun. Idleness is
the root of all evil, so she said. Stitching till my
fingers were sore with it. Spotting the linen, she
said, for I was forever pricking my fingers, being
clumsy at it. And the tears running down my face,
not with the pain of it, but from vexation. Wishing
for other things, I know not what they were. The
young lack patience. And scolding atop the discomfort, my aching fingers, for the blood spots that
would need soaking, and my stitches too large.
Well, she said, Adam and Eve walked naked in the
garden, having no knowledge of their own shame,
and now for our sin we must sew garments just as
soon as we can thread a needle, and stitch shirts
for our masters. Besides, she said, the weather
has turned cold since then, and climes far more
inclement.

Aurea prima sata est aetas. Those who study Latin
are not required to stitch shirts. *Ante mare et terras
et quod tegit omnia caelum unus erat toto naturae . . .*
how does it go on? A little patience, sir, it will come
back to me. My eyesight is not what it was, and my

memory fails me now and then. And I have been unwell this past fortnight. But if you have brought some ancient text with you, I will endeavour to read it. I would not have you think I told an untruth. I am no liar.

I tell the truth, sir, though you whip me for it. I am no thief. I would I knew the meaning of those books, and so escaped stitching. My brother John, now, had he lived, would have sewn no shirts. It is a poor way to lose your eyesight, bringing little reward. A shirt is but a shirt, when all is said and done. But I would not have you think I told an untruth.

I knew the sounds by their letters, though not the meaning. I wish I had known their meaning, and so got something for my trouble. Something about a golden age, I think, without laws to compel, nor fear of punishment. My lady told me, that took me to Ireland. Else I had never known it.

It grows cold, daughter. What is left to burn, now we have no coals? And winter not yet over. The child must be kept warm, but there has been no work this past fortnight. I like not his pallor, husband. I would we had money to buy coals, this house being damp and draughty. Nothing will ease his coughing. Have you not heard him this night? I have scarce slept, for pacing up and down with him. Honey will not soothe it, nor the linctus. Pray for him.

Is that you, daughter? Take my shawl, I would not have you shiver. I shall be well directly. I would not be a burden. Sir, I said, I would live by my own industry, liking not to exist by charity. But he was very kind. Madam, he said, you need no other voucher for whose daughter you are – your face is sufficient testimonial. He would have got me a pension, had he lived. Such kindness in my old age. I had not thought to see it.

How dark it grows. Get us a candle, so we may have light. I have worn out my eyes with stitching, and working by firelight is not good, neither for sight nor stitching. If I had a penny, so she said, for each and every candle he burnt over his books, I would be a fine lady now, with servants of my own. But she let her tongue run away with her upon occasion, thinking long service gave her licence to speak her thoughts. Alas, I fear it did not. Have I told you of her, how she stood by us at the end? I think I did, surely, she being almost a mother to us, that had none.

I will speak out, she said. You may stop my wages but you cannot stop my mouth. And let out such a flood as none could halt. These girls are innocent of wrongdoing, and I must speak for them, that have no other to take their part. And if they had not been, who could blame them? For they are used, and spurned, and sorely tried both day and night, and I have watched it now too long with aching heart. To see such daughters is to know a servant free.

Aye, free to go, she screeched, and father sat, his blind smile on his face, and saying not a word. To have used her so, that served you since a child, and spoke but from devotion. She was like a mother to us, that had none, in her rough way, though flouting sentiment. And sat up late of nights, when he was but a schoolboy, to make sure he got safe to bed when all the world was sleeping, and he must yet be at his studies. Scarce more than a child herself, and hardly able to keep from dozing off, as she would say.

Unlettered as I be, and this she told him, I still can see what's plain as any pikestaff, and needs no tutoring. If love is blind, self-love is blinder far, and you have lacked in duty to your children, that are forever calling them unkind, undutiful to you. Love begets love, she said, and much else in the same vein, and called his wife a scheming harridan, that sought but to serve herself in serving him, who was too blind to know it.

I fear I weep even now to think on it. Forgive my weakness, but the old are foolish, and tears come easily for ancient hurts, that should not pain us now. But such a storm as broke about our heads that day, I never knew till then. Like to the summer's end, when sultry days explode in thunder after long rumblings, and clouds burst out their contents in a cold downpour. From that time on there was no turning back.

Have I been sleeping? Send little Liza to me, and I will teach her her letters. I think she has the gift for learning readily, and must profit from it. I hear that gentlefolk now send their daughters to school, where they learn French, and other tongues. And read rather for pleasure than profit. I should have liked that, had I been born to it. But I was not, though I think on it sometimes, how it might have been otherwise. But the child must learn all she can, though poor, and use those wits she has, and not neglect them. I would we could have done more for you, but there's no use crying over spilt milk, and times were hard. Send her to me. Why is the house so quiet? Are they all outdoors? If the sun shines, I am glad of it. It will do her good, for I know she has been unwell. Sunshine and good country air will do more for body and soul than any physic. I know this from my youth. Did I not tell you of the time we fled to the country?

If we could but afford more candles. I have worn out my eyes with stitching, and working gold thread for rich men's coats, not a task, he said, fit for his children. What was he thinking of, to let you be apprenticed for such work, contrary to principles of faith and politics? To foster luxury by slavish labour, was this a righteous end? Alas, sir, as I told him, he thought not so, else had he taught us in a manner fitting for his heirs. But he despised us, thinking on us as our mother's offspring, not his own, and would be rid of us as nuisances, being less than dutiful. Mr Addison has been most kind. He would have got me a pension, had he lived. Sir, I told him, all my life I have been industrious, and I would be so now, if the means can be got. To live upon charity is not in my nature, but I fear the means desert me. I have had to wear spectacles since a young woman, and am my father's daughter in this. A little in pride also, I must confess, liking not to live upon charity. But beggars must be no choosers.

I am no thief, madam, no, nor ever have been. That you should call it theft when books have gone astray, calling his children to account, and then his servant, shows how you think on us. You would be rid of us, I know. Time for them to earn their daily bread, if they cannot get husbands, I have heard you say this to him oft enough. What should we do, you shrew? Find some old man and turn his daughters out? Calling them thieves, and telling tales, that lack of sight makes easy? Is this the path of womanly virtue you would have us follow? I thank you, madam, but I scorn to sink so low, and if penury must follow, so be it. Besides, I should be hard put to it to find another such, so full of rancour, and so gullible.

I grow hot. This room lacks air. I would have a window open, and drink a little. Even daughters should inherit, and get their patrimony. This is no theft, I think. So my uncle thought, and he the lawyer. He saw us right in the end, using his lawyer's cunning. I have heard him say, it is not just that heads of households should hold absolute sway, as my father thought. Being of the opposite opinion, and thinking ever that Church and state must overrule domestic tyranny, which some called freedom. Wives may be unloved, and daughters disobedient, so he said, and yet must be protected under law. He did humour him but, in so doing, ensured we should inherit.

My cousin Catherine has spoken of this. He was a kind man, my uncle, and would not blow his own trumpet, thinking discretion the better part of valour, and would have no thanks. But I must thank him even so, as must my sisters, for getting us the little that was our due. He knew, you see, that, as he put it, where there was no will there was no way for his own children to be disinherited, and all left to his wife. And so he let my father babble on, each time he called, and seemed to humour him in his designs, knowing that, if he put not pen to paper, the will would surely fall, as proved the case. The court refused her probate, though she got a spiteful servant, who never knew us, to speak ill of us in court. He being neither sick nor dying at the time, there should have been a written testament. My uncle Christopher, since he was a lawyer, had always known this, and, had he thought it right, could have forestalled the outcome, but did nothing.

It was but little, and yet I must be thankful for it. Your father married me when I had nothing, no dowry to my name. I was glad to bring a little, when it came, to help our early struggles. He sent back my mother, the dowry being unpaid. So my grandam told us. Let them have their mother's dowry, nought else – I hear he spoke thus at the last. Meaning we should have nothing. Poor father, so mean of soul in petty matters, it fits not to his gift, that God did give him. I would speak of him only with reverence, as the world does. And we must be thankful for it, relieving, as it does, our penury. I would speak truth, but speak it kindly. I have long since forgiven.

You had a good father, daughter. He took me when I had nothing, in honest affection, and never sought to reproach me for it in after years. If thou dost bring as much in fondness as I bear for thee, then I am rich indeed. So he spoke. I think I wept, daughter, to hear such words, uttered so kindly. I was not used to it. He was a father to me, then a friend, and such a husband as I trust you have in yours, a helpmate ever.

And yet, I think you have. Is he not a weaver also? Do not marry above your station, for it is a sure way to be contemned. As our old servant used to say, when Adam delved and Eve span, neither could read Latin. We are to be kept ignorant, I think, to keep us in servitude.

But I am my father's daughter for all that. Mr Addison had no doubts in the matter, when first he saw me. Madam, he said, your face is sufficient testimonial. *Aurea prima sata est aetas.* I will recollect how it goes on, if you but give me a moment. My memory, like my eyesight, begins to fail me. It was the lady who took me to Ireland with her who first told me something of the meaning. Before that I would recite but parrot fashion. My poor child, she would say, for, though hired to be her companion, she did ever treat me like a daughter, having promised this to him who should have done so . . . you do but squall like a parrot, that hath no soul, and thus no understanding. But you have both, and so you must endeavour . . . how did she speak to me? . . . and so you must endeavour, against all odds, to seek the understanding men would yet deny you. Such a lady, I never knew her like. She put me on my mettle, as no one else. Are you a silly bird, or are you human? I hear her still. It had to do with that first golden age, as I remember, as ancients saw it.

It grieved me to be despised by him, I do confess. I am no silly bird, sir, no, and pride, I fear, burns in my veins, even though deemed sinful in a woman. I have seen my sister lash out sarcastical as ever he could be, and that without schooling, or benefit of higher learning. Well, blood runs thicker than water, as they say, and we might have given him cause for pride, had he but looked upon us differently.

How a man looks upon his children, now there's a mystery. It is quite otherwise with us women, for we know them to be flesh of our flesh, though opposite in gender. Heir to all our ills, and helpless at the start, like to fall sick, and die, and keep us wakeful with their crying in the night. Which of us has not paced the floor, and kissed his tiny cheeks, and felt our hearts grow cold within us at such fragility? And should we then think them a different breed, for that they have a little tassel dangling betwixt their legs? But they are taken from us, if

137

they live, and must be turned to men. And so turned from us, as I believe.

It is not the custom to speak of such things, but there is none to hear us. Besides, I am old, and I think I am not long for this world. I have felt so strange of late, as though I drift between my former selves and myself as I am now. I thought I spoke to your father but a little time ago, yet I know he is dead long since. I think I will be with him presently, and he but beckons. And I am ready, else I would not hear him. The Lord is merciful, and I shall see my babes again, that caused me so much sorrow.

So will you, daughter, when your time is come. Be sure of it, though you grieve now, and find but little comfort in the thought. I would not have you weep. I heard your father's voice as I was dozing, as clear and strong as though he stood within this room, and he did tell it me. Your babes do live, and you shall know them, as you know me that speaks. Is it not strange? But so it was. I feel such sureness now, as never yet. For I inhabit different times and places, and move as easily as any ghost or spirit, belonging nowhere. And so will you.

Is it night now? I think I must have slept too long. Why did you not wake me? No matter, I will get up presently and do what I can, once this weakness leaves me. I would not be a burden. You have cares enough as it is. I know it. I have lived as you do, and I know how it is. But my mother, dying at my birth, I never saw her. And so I did not tend her when she was old. Think you she will know me, and I her, when all souls are risen from sleep? And yet I have dreamt of her, from time to time, both lately and long ago, and always knew her for who she was. I cannot tell you how she looked, except that she seemed fond, and tender, and quite unlike his last wife. I knew her not by outward shows, which in dreams are oft belied by other forms of knowing, as though the outer form were variable, but not the inner spirit, which shines forth, and so declares itself. How will my babes look, think you? Will they know me in like manner?

A little broth will give me strength. I would teach Liza her letters, she has the aptitude for it. My little Lucy died of the cough, else she might have done well at her books. I never quarrelled with your father, except in this. He thought I set too much value on book learning, he being all for practical matters, and keeping of accounts, and such like skills. Let them help in the shop, he said, and wind quills. And yet you are as poor now as ever I was, being wedded to a weaver. Honesty will not suffice, nor hard work.

Not a man in the family I came from ever laboured with his hands, but was sent to school, and studied, and was turned to a gentleman, that need not bother his head on a falling off in trade, or foreign imports that do take the bread from out our mouths. My father should have gone into the Church, but found another course, despising it. As for my uncle, he did study law. Now that's a way to live and die in comfort. Daughters must have dowries, or else go down in the world.

Or marry an old man with desires no lower than his stomach. That is the way to make old bones. They say she still lives, the termagant, and is as sparing now with her pennies as ever she was. Too mean with her breath to die, as the saying goes. And yet I would not quarrel with her, not now, for all her scolding. A shrew is not born, but made so, and I doubt she was content. I know this now, being old. We are creatures of circumstance, and I have not always been so forbearing as I should have been. I know this and, if I have caused you grief through lack of patience, I ask you to forgive me. It is a sovereign virtue, but hard to practise, though we be women. Confess it, is it not so? I think I should find it easier to wield a sword, show bravery, or any attributes deemed manly, than dull old patience, which is rather seen by what is not, than any presence, positive and sure. And yet we must endeavour to be patient, a quality that by its very nature is measured out in years, not hours. The briefest falling off will smirch our virtue, whilst heroes lie at rest.

I shall be well by and by, do not fret. I need but to get my strength, for nothing ails me. Why do you not send the child to me, and I will instruct her? Besides, I like to have her by me, she prattles so sweetly. Loving women do not make old bones, she would say, when mocked of her long spinster-hood. I speak now of our old servant. And yet she was like a mother to us, that had none, though her rough ways would deny it. She spoke up for us at the last, and so lost her livelihood. For I am honest, so she did declare, and to speak honestly I think you are not so, for you are bent on seeing evil where there is none, this being most oft in the eye of the beholder, as I do think, for you would rob these motherless girls of the little they do have, and so you call them robbers. A book may go astray, and so may pence, without that they be stolen. But a birthright stolen, or honest reputation taken away by idle tittletattle, that's a theft indeed, and you are guilty of it, so I think, in speaking thus.

You should have heard her, banging pots and

pans the while in furious clatter, so all the world could hear it. Such a din from out the nether regions, it reached up to the study, kept silent and secure. Pandemonium, my father called it, delighting in the word, though little else.

I saw her weep that day, though only tears of rage, her face flushed crimson that a servant should speak thus, and flout authority. She never wept otherwise, I think, being too much the shrew for tenderness, or womanly sorrow. Well, loving women do not make old bones, and she must be ancient indeed now, in her long widowhood. I wish her joy of it, these tedious years. I doubt if they be joyous. Coddle your cold bones, aye, your cold heart, by a warm hearth. I must pity rather than hate you now.

We should die having made peace with our enemies, that could not live in friendship with our neighbours. Forgive us our trespasses, as we forgive them that trespass against us. Such a pandemonium, he said, for she flew up to him at once, in outrage. He would have quietness at any price, I think. And so he heard but her voice, which was shrill enough, and heard no other. Buying tranquillity, though dearly bought. No rights but his, no argument but hers, that catered for his needs, a tranquil household.

Else how could he send her from him, letting her be dismissed, that had served him since childhood, though but a child herself, when in his mother's house? And all the years since then. To let her go so. I think she loved us, though she spoke not of it. I know so. I would that I had put my arms about her more often, and told her my affection. As a child I did it, when she gave me sugar plums, or wiped my tears. But she was never one for such displays, and losing infancy we lose the gift of showing our affection, and taking in return the love that's given. Get off with you, she'd say, for I have work to do, and hot air never yet made dumplings. She would give me raisins, my head being little higher than the table, and call me duck, and tell me stories of her father's farm, which she could scarce recall, being so young when put to service. Her skin did smell of onions, I remember, and when I smell them now upon my hands, I think of her.

I have looked upstairs and down, father, but I cannot find it. I think, with so much moving, it must be mislaid. What am I to do, father, will you not hear something else? No, sir, I know a book is not like a pudding, so you may eat rhubarb in place of plums, but it cannot be found. Mary is not in the house, so I cannot ask her. I read from it only last week, at your behest, I know, but now I cannot find it. Has someone other read from it for you? It will be found in time but, though I have searched high and low, I cannot see it. A book having no legs, as you say, it cannot walk out the house by itself. Did you lend it to someone? Then it must be within doors.

No, father, who should have sold it, and for why? She would do no such thing and, besides, she cannot read. No, nor the dunghill women neither. I think you have been speaking with my stepmother, else you would not accuse her of such a deed, nor us. I would buy you another, gladly, but I have no money of my own. Nor have my sisters. Is it then valuable? I thought we were poor, and yet so much for a book, and then so many of them. The house so full, there is scarce room for us.

But I am no thief, sir. You do wrong us.

She says the dust in them brings plague, and will shift them about no more. Besides, since she cannot read, how is she to put them back just so? They are all as Greek to her, even if in Latin or her mother tongue. So though you cry order, order, it is of little use. But a thief, father, how could you think it, after such long service?

So we must be her eyes, and help her to it. Such scheming. But I mean not my sisters, I mean your wife. Who would be rid of us. Like the false cuckoo she is, emptying the nest of fledglings. Though they be honest, and your own. She it is who has been pouring poison in your ear, else you could never suppose such devious plots, and credit such designs within your house. Because we are but women, father, deceitful as Delilah? And yet our step-mother's a woman too. As your honest servant was wont to say: there's none so blind as they who will not see.

I have seen her burn papers for kindling, it is true, but this is no theft, but ignorance. And yet, I think, she had enough wits to make a scholar, were she born your brother. And more than enough homespun wisdom to make a preacher, though you laugh at it. As she would say, you get from a vessel what you put into it, no more.

How cold it grows in this room. We must have coal, else the child will get sick. It was catching cold that took Isaac from us when he was six months old, for all his swaddling. Though, to tell the truth, he was born sickly, and I never knew an hour from his birth that was not fearful and full of dread. Did I tell you of it? I hope you may be spared such sorrow, for I think it is harder far to bear when they live beyond childbed, and look upon your face, and learn to smile, and know your voice. To go through the valley of the shadow, and then be bereft, it requires more fortitude than I am mistress of, and a humbler spirit. Yet I have tried to be a good Christian, thanking God for His mercies.

I pray you may be more fortunate. You have a good husband, though he is poor. Better a dinner of green herbs, where love is, than a stalled ox and hatred with it. I have known both, child, and I know whereof I speak. Yet we must have coals, else the child will take sick.

Is it night, and the child gone to bed? You must keep her at her lessons, for she is bright as the morning star, and quick to learn. I would I had been half so quick, for I might have gone further, and not stumbled. And yet, not so. There are those who are made stupid by education. We have been spared this, being poor, and female besides. Having our arses flogged to quicken sluggish brains, whether we would learn or no. Construing Latin by the hour. Useless lumber, your father called it. For learning is not wisdom, and would have us foolish for speaking merely in our mother tongue. This is the privilege by which they rule.

Aurea prima sata est aetas. Yet I do know a little, if you will hear me. I am no liar, sir. I was compelled to it, as were my sisters. Anne was excused, for she did stammer. *Quae vindice nullo . . .* it will come to me, and others also, if you would hear me. My eyesight now is poor, but memory serves. *Poena metusque aberant . . .* You are very good, sir, to take an interest in my plight.

Let her keep accounts, and do arithmetic. Your father was much in favour of this, as mine was also. A shilling not put down in the book was a shilling stolen, which could be wellnigh a hanging matter. So let her do sums, else there will be discord in her household. Write down, it was spent on flour and candles, so harmony shall reign.

It was spent on flour and candles, father, I will swear to it on the good Book. She knows it, and seeks but to stir the pot. But I would be at peace with you, and settle accounts at last. So much commotion for a mere trifle! I would lie in my bed without strife, and sleep easy.

Think you we shall sleep without dreams, to kiss and make amends in Heaven? We should do so in this world, and so leave it in amity, and quietness. The young may die otherwise, which is their peril, but those who are old should first settle all accounts, and so go peacefully. Such a pother for a shilling gone astray, and the whole house topsyturvy when the book could not be found. But she would blow upon the coals, and it were in Hell.

Well, there are those who think that the old Adam is in every man, aye, and grandmother Eve also, and the story of our first fall but a parable, of greed and suchlike vices. I have read this somewhere in my youth. My husband showed it me. The old Adam is in every man, of greed and tyranny, and Paradise shall come again when the earth is a common treasury, each man taking that which will provide sufficiency, but no more. For property, and buying and selling of land, is the curse upon us. As if the earth were made peculiarly for them, that have got it by violence or cunning, and enforced people to pay them money for what should be a public use. We are a long way now from such thoughts, and yet I think there is some truth in them, and reason also.

Is it morning yet? We must be up before sunrise,

if it is winter, for there is much work to do. Did not the cock crow? To tell the truth, I thought myself wellnigh in Paradise, the year we went into the country to escape the plague. I was never so happy, and would be out of doors before the cock. And see the dawn come up, a wondrous sight for someone from the city, forever in a smother.

Though it was but a few short months in all, it shines forth in my memory of girlhood as though it were wellnigh the better part of it, and counted in years. Is it not ever thus, memory playing strange tricks on us, so the grey years leave not a jot behind, but one day's sunshine suffusing all? The years since Mr Clarke died, and Caleb took ship for India, what has become of them, can you tell me? 'Tis all like a grey fog, and grey in my hair to prove it, each hour like the one before it, much of a muchness. If there are landmarks, they do drift within it, uneasily, having no firm foundation on solid ground. I have lost my husband, and since then much else, as those who grow old must do. And yet some hours shine in the dark like jewels, though half a century lies in between. I think it is God's grace, to comfort us, so we may know the promise that waits for us in Heaven.

If Paradise should be as those green fields of England long ago, and muddy lanes, and rampant hedgerows, twisted apple trees, I should be well content. Our little Liza would soon be well if she could run free in such sweet air. It is not good for infants, the foul stench of our city streets. They thrive like country crops, and so grow strong. And yet, we must earn our livelihood in this plague pit, there's no help for it, though soot besmirch fresh linen before it is dry, and brings on the cough.

I would our little Lizzie might run in the meadows

as I did once, and lie on her back to watch the skylark soar, and clouds float by. When you were sick I told him, Mr Clarke, if we could but get this child some good country air, and herbs still wet with dew of a May morning, then I am certain it would thrive. I thought you would die like the others, if the truth be told.

If wishes were horses, he said, then beggars would ride. Besides, he said, you talk but old wives' gossip, and God's will is done as surely in country as in city, despite our travail. I thank God you lived, and yet I think your Liza would benefit from going out of town.

If it rained, I have no memory of it. We were packed tight as oysters in a barrel, the house being so small, yet out of doors was all the world to roam in. You must accept His will, daughter, and not weep. The child is in God's keeping. But summer must have an end, and winter follow. I thought I should never cease from fretting when we returned, the plague having abated. Not just for the hedgerows, and the birds singing, no, though that was well enough, but to be free as the wind that blows, heeding no master, no hourly duty, that was a wondrous gift I never knew till then, nor found it since. There being fewer books to try us, fewer tasks, and far more space for refuge.

Well, we must all leave our Eden, is it not so, and be thrust out of Paradise, though the brief taste of it do haunt us ever, and will not leave our thoughts. So sorrow follows joy, and is the deeper for it. This is our trial, I think, to know from whence we came, and find no path by which we may return.

God grant us faith to find it, in this our wilderness. For we have need of Him. I see it yet, the skylark, how it rose in perfect freedom, and hear it

147

singing. I think the Lord allows us such a sign, a memory such as this, so far, and yet so clear, to be for us a beacon in the night when we are lost, glowing on a distant hillside. I would return, and see what I saw then. You shall come with me, and get the wind upon your face. It will cure you fast enough. I like not your colour, no.

Dry your eyes, child, and we will go. There are poppies growing, and the clouds run like sheep in the sky. You will see it, and grow strong, and tall as an oak. Your father knows nothing, no. Gold will not cure it, nor physic, if my soul sickens. It pants for air and light in which to grow. Money will not heal it, nor sternest discipline, though I obey.

I thought I should never be done with grieving, back at Bunhill, and it a plague pit, and walled in, though there were trees enough, and green spaces, and windmills turning merrily. But I had lost that which I had but lately found, and knew myself bereft. To taste such heady fruit and then to be deprived, it wounds the spirit. From that time forth I served unwillingly, forever in a pet, nursing an ill humour at every given task, and longed to run away, as once I could, and hear the silence and my brooding thoughts, and speak with nobody.

It was the Devil that was in me, so she said, our stepmother. Why, she was well enough till now, but takes after her sister, and mimics her, having no better model. Another time she'd say it was my age, I being then fourteen or thereabouts, the mother rising in me, female humours stirring, or some such thing. All but the thing itself, a wild and unschooled spirit which, having tasted freedom, craved for it.

Was it the serpent spoke to me? I know not. If so, then I have had a lifetime to repent, in bitterness and sorrow. I have brought forth children in pain and misery, and buried them again. You know this, as you know how we must serve, changing a father for a husband, and look to him. I have been forgiven, I think, my husband being a kind man, and loving.

Lavender grew by the wall. I would sleep with it under my pillow, to bring sweet dreams. I cannot think it was the Devil, for all her scolding. And yet, I wished her ill. She read it, being no fool, in my black looks, at Bunhill. Such dreams as it brought me, who knows whether for good or ill? Beguiled by fleshly things, and by the spirit. For the scent of new-mown hay I would have done such things, I know not, nor cared, if not found out.

But if God sees all things, I am lost, if joy of such a kind is sinful. And earthly things. To disobey, I know it is a sin, but what of conscience? If God speaks in the skylark, must I not hear him? And hear him in my blood, which likewise speaks? Such confusion as I felt, I feel it yet. Honour thy father and thy mother, this we must surely do. And yet Jesus has spoken otherwise, telling us to leave them.

Is that you, father, knocking on the floor with your stick? How dark it grows, and you in haste. I know not where I put the candle, and cannot find it. I will come as quickly as I can, though my fingers are stiff with the cold in them, so I can scarce hold a pen. And when I heard an owl screech in the night, though it was but an owl, she swore it was poor souls in the plague pit, crying for Christian burial. Being tumbled in like cattle, they could not rest. It is not healthy in this city, I would we had not returned.

We shall have rest at last, I know it, and sleep till

Judgement comes. I could rest now, were it not for the knocking. Will he not sleep in his grave like other men? My children, though they cried in the night often enough, they do not wake me now. This is a strange thing indeed.

And yet, though books may carry contagion, they do not die of it. Not as our children do. And so we are judged. God gave you a great gift indeed, when he took away your eyes, else had you seen much that is ugly. It is we, with our eyes, that are in the dark. And so I must find the candle.

That the fire should spare us also, it was a sign of His favour. So he would have it. For it came within sight and sound of our windows, and marred the hangings. I could smell it long after, though we aired the rooms. But if the air itself be full of soot, washing and hanging out will do no good. As our old servant said, only so much can be done by hard labour and honest housekeeping, and if the air be foul 'tis no use fanning. For which she was called impudent.

Such a commotion I never saw before nor since. And Mistress Betty was for moving our chattels out of the house, as neighbours had begun to do, the wind blowing in our direction. And my father said never mind the few chairs and fewer garments, it was his books we should be stacking out of doors. Aye, said our servant, and there they will make a pretty bonfire, God willing. And madam our stepmother asked her to explain her meaning, knowing how she had but little liking for them. I mean only, she said, that they are as like to burn out of doors as in, if a cart cannot be got to take them further afield. But yet we were spared, and the books likewise.

The booksellers who did remove their wares to

the vaults of St Paul for safekeeping lost all when the church burned. I remember it was much spoken of.

Is it daylight yet? I dreamt I lay in the orchard, hearing the insects hum about me, and the smell of ripe fruit strong in my nostrils, and thought myself in Heaven. I was filled with such sweet content, and yet so airy light, I knew I dreamt. Think you it will be so, and we shall find our dearest moments in eternity? I could wish it. And yet we have fustian thoughts, and lack vision. Our eyes are too much on stitching, and scouring pots, to know the Holy City.

But I have thought, upon occasion, that both are with us daily. The best and worst, both Heaven and Hell, if you will. I have no learning, but I think we may hope for quietness, and rest, since God is mercy.

Come closer, daughter, I would see your face. You are much like my sister, who died long ago. You never knew her, else you would have loved her gentle spirit. I shall see her, I think, but whole, and no more crippled. An end to pain is a good end, and should suffice us, if the Heavenly City be long in coming, to open up its gates. Have no fear, child, for God is merciful, and will deal more kindly with you at the Judgement-seat than ever men will do upon this earth.

It comforts me to have you near. I would I had known my mother. I ever tried to be a loving parent, thinking the world harsh enough when we are grown. It was no uncommon thing in my youth to hate a parent, being roughly used. But I would rather my little ones should know what it is to be cherished, than to learn in a hard school, and be made hardy for the life that follows. To have known a little joy in youth, and loving comfort, this is a lantern to us all our days, and brings light on a winter's night.

For the young are innocent, I think. Though we are all born in sin, and must bear the fault that comes from our first parents, there is a kind of goodness, a purity, that should not be marred. I doubt that beatings and harsh words will make of them good Christians. Such a comely child you were, with your blonde locks. It was a miracle to me that you lived, having lost so many. I am thankful to God you were spared, to show me some kindness in my old age. A mother dotes, as you know full well, tied by the bond of flesh, and every little fever makes her fearful. I thought I should lose you once. Your face hectic, and coughing through the night. A father, being less bound, can be more stern, and mete out punishment like the God of the Israelites that Moses knew.

Still no daylight? I could drink a little now. But this is tea – have we then come into riches? Or did Caleb send it us? I should like to have seen him once more, but they tell me he is dead, and buried far off. The world is changing, that we drink tea now. I am used to small beer, and not much else, though I care not for it.

Let me sip a little more, for my mouth is dry. Our little Liza is dead, is she not? I thought as much. There is a kind of silence in the house, that speaks of it. I see you weep. You must not do so, for she is now with God, and in His love. And yet it is hard, I know, for a woman to think so. Men speak such comfort easily enough, having not endured the pangs that we must suffer. Yet when their schemes do founder they are not resigned. Chimeras, dreams, these are their hard-born children, that they would not see die, but rather fight and suffer. Though half the world must suffer with them, they will on. But we must be resigned, and bear our sorrow, it being the will of God. Child, His wisdom is a mystery that cannot now be fathomed. But at the last all will be made light, as we enter into His glory.

It is nearly morning, and I will get up soon. I feel easier now. Put back the shutters. I did hear the cock crow in Bedfordshire. You must dry your eyes. It will pass, this present pain, believe me. I have been where you are now, and know this to be so. Time is a great physician, as they say, and cures all ills. It is a harsh school, this life of ours, is it not? And when we have done learning, our time is run. I would we could learn it from books, and pass *cum laude* as our betters think to do.

And yet they fool themselves, that think so. For we are all born ignorant, and must learn by our errors, that is the pity of it. I think, though they speak of two, that the tree of knowledge and the tree of life are but one and the same, and in eating the fruit of one we must taste the other. If this be heresy, I plead guilty.

Will you not get my gown? I feel refreshed, and would wash my face. I thought I knew it once, in a country orchard, all that God would have us know. But no doubt I was foolish, being a young girl. And yet, if conscience is our yardstick, then I heard His voice, and knew His wisdom. Such a stillness, child, I never knew till then, nor found it since. In which the trees did whisper, as in awe, feeling the breath of God upon them. So I thought. And listened to His Word. I heard the insects hum, and mine own heart within me. He told me, peace.

Hearing no more, I knew He told me this. I would I might have stood thus for all eternity, and nothing alter.

How long ago was this? I was but thirteen years of age, and now I am old. And yet I see it clear as though it were yesterday. Is this not strange? And so it has no end, though time did pass, and all things alter with it. The sun shines up above, and I am young. The apple tastes sweet in my mouth, I taste it still, and hear the bees hum. It is a sign, I know, of how our souls will fare, within His mercy.

Now it is morning I must go about my business. I have spoken of this to no one, in all these years. For to see such a vision, and speak of it, is to invite mockery. Or unwelcome fame. Though I am my father's daughter, I must keep silent. He would not wish me to speak thus, it being thought unfitting. Say nothing of it to him, I beg of you. I dread his scornful tongue. And I would not have her know where I go. I shall be scolded for idleness. And yet I do what is necessary, no task undone. But some other will always be found, if I stay. This is the way of it, being ever at their beck and call. And so I hid in the orchard, to find myself at last. Finding Him also, so I think, but durst not tell of it.

I feel light of spirit now, all my pain is gone. *Aurea prima* . . . they say there was a golden age once, before men fell from grace. Could we but return . . . But, I think, there was never living without struggle, else had we been feeble, and not fit.

Blow out the candle, daughter. It is morning. I would not have us waste the hours. Such a long night as this has been, but now I see daylight. Give me your hand, and I will take you with me to the orchard. You will taste the fruit.